WORKSKILLS
Book 1

Mary Lou Beilfuss Byrne

Consulting Authors

Susan C. Quatrini
Kathy S. Van Ormer

Prentice Hall

Upper Saddle River, New Jersey 07458

Library of Congress Cataloging-in-Publication Data
Byrne, Mary Lou Beilfuss, (date)
Workskills,. Book 1/Mary Lou Beilfuss Byrne ; Consulting authors, Susan C. Quatrini, Kathy S. Van Ormer.
p. cm.
ISBN 0-13-953076-2 (pb) :
1. English language--Textbooks for foreign speakers. I. Quatrini, Susan C., (date). II. Van Ormer, Kathy S., (date) III. Title. IV. Title: Workskills book 1. V. Title : Workskills book one.
PE1128.B88 1994 93-24766
428.2'4--dc20 CIP

Acquisitions Editor: Nancy Leonhardt
Managing Editor: Sylvia Moore
Editorial Production/Supervision: Shirley Hinkamp
Pre-Press Production: Infinite Graphics
Cover Illustration: Comstock
Cover Design: Laura Ierardi
Copy Editor: Anne Graydon
Prepress Buyer: Ray Keating
Manufacturing Buyer: Lori Bulwin

Printed in the United States of America

10 9 8

ISBN 0-13-953076-2

Prentice-Hall International (UK) Limited, *London*
Prentice-Hall of Australia Pty. Limited, *Sydney*
Prentice-Hall Canada Inc., *Toronto*
Prentice-Hall Hispanoamericana, S.A., *Mexico*
Prentice-Hall of India Private Limited, *New Delhi*
Prentice-Hall of Japan, Inc., *Tokyo*
Pearson Education Asia Pte. Ltd., *Singapore*
Editora Prentice-Hall do Brasil, Ltda., *Rio de Janeiro*

Contents

About the Book vii

UNIT 1 Company Policies (*punctuality*)

Before You Read 1
Reading About Work—"Juan's Traffic Trouble" 2
  Understanding New Words 2
  Understanding the Reading 3
Discussing 3
Reading at Work—Reading a Company Policy Manual 5
  Understanding New Words 5
  Understanding the Reading 6
Writing 6
Listening 7
Reading Charts and Using Math 9

UNIT 2 Giving/Following Directions and Instructions (*demonstrating comprehension of multi-step directions*)

Before You Read 10
Reading About Work—"Kim and the Golden Dragon" 11
  Understanding New Words 11
  Understanding the Reading 12
Discussing 13
Reading at Work—Reading an Employee's Checklist 14
  Understanding New Words 14
  Understanding the Reading 15
Writing 16
Listening 16
Using Math *(adding decimals, calculating percents)* 18

UNIT 3 Safety (*signs and labels*)

Before You Read 21
Reading About Work—"Sylvia's Safe Skies" 22
  Understanding New Words 23
  Understanding the Reading 24
Discussing 25
Reading at Work—Reading Safety Signs and Labels 27
  Understanding New Words 27
  Understanding the Reading 28
Writing 28
Listening 29
Using Math and a Bar Graph 30

UNIT 4 **Interacting with Co-workers (*using first and last names, familiarity*)**

Before You Read 32
Reading About Work—"Small Talk at Freddy's Finest Foods" 33
Understanding New Words 34
Understanding the Reading 35
Discussing 36
Reading at Work—Reading Employee Notices on the Bulletin Board 37
Understanding New Words 37
Understanding the Reading 39
Writing 39
Listening 40
Using Math (*estimating numbers, adding decimals*) 41

UNIT 5 **Interacting with Supervisors (*formal/informal forms of address*)**

Before You Read 42
Reading About Work—"Welcome to the Sleepy Hollow Hotel" 43
Understanding New Words 44
Understanding the Reading 45
Discussing 46
Reading at Work—Reading a Company Memo 48
Understanding New Words 48
Understanding the Reading 49
Writing 49
Listening 50
Using Math (*solving word problems, determining when to add, subtract, multiply, or divide*) 51

UNIT 6 **Personalities and Conflicts (*getting along with co-workers*)**

Before You Read 52
Reading About Work—"Production Problems at Epic Electronics" 53
Understanding New Words and Phrases 54
Understanding the Reading 55
Discussing 56
Reading at Work—10 Steps to Solve Problems 57
Understanding New Words 57
Understanding the Reading 58
Writing 58
Listening 59
Using Math and a Line Graph 60

UNIT 7 **Valued Work Behaviors/Qualities (*dependability, responsibility*)**

Before You Read 62
Reading About Work—"Susan's Special Night" 63
Understanding New Words 64
Understanding the Reading 65
Discussing 66
Reading at Work—Reading a Company Newsletter 67
Understanding New Words 67
Understanding the Reading 68
Writing 68
Listening 69
Using Math and a Bar Graph 70

UNIT 8 **Job Performance (*quality of work, recognition of service*)**

Before You Read 72
Reading About Work—"Eva's Evaluation" 73
Understanding New Words 74
Understanding the Reading 75
Discussing 76
Reading at Work—Reading an Employee Evaluation Form 77
Understanding New Words 77
Understanding the Reading 79
Writing 79
Listening 80
Using Math and Reading a Paycheck Stub 81

UNIT 9 **Goal Setting (*short-term goals, evaluation of goal attainment*)**

Before You Read 83
Reading About Work—"Gilberto Sets Goals" 84
Understanding New Words 85
Understanding the Reading 86
Discussing 87
Reading at Work—Reading a Posted Job Opening 89
Understanding New Words 89
Understanding the Reading 90
Writing 90
Listening 91
Using Math *(solving problems using multiplication and division)* 92

UNIT 10 Job Training/Continuing Education (*lifelong learning*)

Before You Read 93
Reading About Work—"Clara's Computer Classes" 94
Understanding New Words 95
Understanding the Reading 96
Discussing 97
Reading at Work—Reading a Company Memo 98
Understanding New Words 98
Understanding the Reading 100
Writing 100
Listening 101
Using Math and a Pie Chart 103

Audio Tape Scripts 106

Skills Index 119

About the Book

Brief Description of *Workskills*

Workskills is a series of three books and three audiotapes for workplace literacy. The books and tapes are written for students at high beginning (Students are literate.), low intermediate, and high intermediate levels. The books and tapes are coordinated so that they can be used with multi-level groups of students and one teacher. Each book deals with different aspects of the same unit topic.

The approach of the texts is functional, contextual, and problem-solving. The exercises are interactive, cooperative, and practical.

Reading, vocabulary development, speaking, listening, and writing are included. The readings are controlled in length and structure. Basic math skills and graphical literacy are included. Positive work attitudes are developed.

Features of *Workskills*

Each unit contains these features:

- Before You Read
- a titled story or dialogue based on the unit theme
- Understanding New Words
- Understanding the Reading
- Discussing
- Reading at Work (including Understanding New Words, a nonfictional reading related to types of reading required at work, and Understanding the Reading)
- Writing
- Listening
- Using Math or Using Graphical Literacy

Teaching with *Workskills*

Before You Read

The unit opening page contains one or more photographs, one or more illustrations, or one or more cartoon frames related to the unit theme. Students examine the photos/illustrations/cartoons and describe what they see. The instructor may wish to list vocabulary suggested by the students. The students continue to work with partners to read, think about and answer the questions on the page. This process helps build on existing vocabulary, relates real work experiences to the lesson, and prepares the students for the reading that follows.

Reading About Work

The **Reading About Work** section includes a fictional story or dialogue that follows the **Before You Read** page and illustrates the unit theme. The stories or dialogues proceed from simple sentences, verb tenses, and grammatical structures to more complex sentences, verb tenses, and grammatical structures. The length of the stories or dialogues gradually increases to help students prepare for the succeeding *Workskills* book(s). The authors chose story settings that represent a variety of workplace situations and/or settings that most students would be familiar with.

Understanding New Words

This feature helps expand and use new vocabulary that was introduced in context in the story or dialogue. Various formats were used throughout *Workskills* to help students find, understand, and practice the new or unfamiliar vocabulary. This section can be used successfully either before or after the story or dialogue, depending on the instructor's preference and the needs of the students.

Understanding the Reading

This feature helps both students and teacher check literal and inferential comprehension of the story or dialogue. Once again, various formats were used in *Workskills* to create and maintain interest. These exercises may be done independently as an assessment, or with a partner or a small group, thus providing more speaking practice.

Discussing

The Discussing portion of the unit provides opportunities for the students to work together on specific activities relating to the story or dialogue and to the unit topic. Students may be asked to complete a conversation, to role play situations they may encounter at the workplace, to solve problems, to evaluate and judge reasons for being late for work, to judge appropriate and inappropriate statements in conversations, etc.

Listening

Each unit of *Workskills* includes a listening activity. The conversations that correspond to the listening activities in the books are found on the accompanying audiotapes for *Workskills* 1,2,3. The types of conversations included are ones that students might hear at work or participate in at work. Most of the conversations involve two co-workers, a supervisor and a worker, or two supervisors. The conversations involve people discussing work-related topics or making "small talk" at work.

The students' tasks in most cases is to listen for specific information. They will need to use this information for various further activities—to fill in a chart or grid, circle or write an answer, take notes, or make judgments. Many times at work, employees are given information that they need to act on. Thus, in some of the listening activities, the students will use the information for further problem-solving activities.

The speech in the conversations is natural and idiomatic. The students will learn that they don't need to understand every word when they are listening for specific information. The exercises will help train the students to pick out only the information pertinent to the task and will also assist them in understanding spoken English in on-the-job situations.

Reading at Work

The Reading at Work section in each unit focuses on the types of readings that an employee might actually encounter on the job: signs, memos, notices on bulletin boards, excerpts from policy and safety manuals, and excerpts from company newsletters. Many of the readings are authentic—at times, they have been modified for the level of Workskills in which they are included.

A variety of comprehension activities follows the readings. These include exercises involving literal and inferential comprehension, making judgments and scanning for specific information. Discussion questions relating the readings to the students' jobs are also included. Whenever possible, the instructor should bring in authentic reading materials from the students' worksite. These added realia will personalize the topic and help the employee to understand his company and his job better.

Writing

These materials are designed to teach English through an integrated skills approach. The writing exercises in the texts generally follow the reading, speaking and listening activities and build upon the previous exercises. The writing exercises are controlled either through format and structure (filling in words, using forms, etc.), or a model is provided with the exercise. Students should be encouraged to draw freely from the model when writing.

The authors also recommend using pre-writing strategies such as brain-storming for ideas and vocabulary, reviewing the reading with a focus on finding specific vocabulary or grammatical structures, group discussion about the writing task, and having the instructor or other class members create a model. The writing assignment may be done as an individual, partner, or group activity.

Using Math and Graphs

The *Workskills* texts include a basic math and graphical skills component in each unit. These exercises were designed to enhance basic skills and meet basic job and personal math needs for the student. The units focus on problems that students will encounter either at work or in their daily lives. Successful completion of all these exercises should prepare students for most basic uses of math in the workplace. Supplemental practice and additional exercises may be necessary for students with limited mathematical background or those who will need a higher level of proficiency on their jobs.

Acknowledgments

We wish to thank the following people:

Elizabeth Minicz
Roseanne Mendoza
Sheila McMillen
Anne Riddick
Rosemary Palicki
Marilyn Antonik

We are also grateful to our students at

Barrett Bindery
C-Line Office Products
College of DuPage
Filtran
Johnson & Quin
Navistar International
Oakton Community College
Panek Precision
Schwake Stone Co.
Triton College

Dedicated to my husband, Jim Byrne, and my children, Christopher Byrne and Jenna Byrne.

With gratitude to Bill and Anne Beilfuss for their unconditional love and never-ending confidence in me.

UNIT 1 *Company Policies*

Before You Read

(making predictions, relating experiences to reading, establishing prior knowledge)

Ken Karp

Look at the picture.

Talk about this picture with a partner.

Read the questions.

Write your answers on the lines.

1. What time of day is it? ______________________________
2. Where are the people in the cars going? ______________________
3. What is a *traffic jam?* ______________________________
4. When were you in a traffic jam? ______________________

Reading About Work

Juan's Traffic Trouble

Juan Lopez has a new job at a factory. It is ten miles from his home. Today is his first day. Juan is a little nervous and too excited to eat breakfast. He drinks coffee, listens to the radio, and makes his lunch. He leaves at 6:15. Work starts at 7:00.

Two miles from home, Juan has a problem. There is a traffic jam. The cars move very slowly. It takes ten minutes to drive one mile. Juan worries he will be late on his first day of work. He changes lanes. He honks his horn at the cars in front of him. He is angry about the traffic. He starts to sweat. The minutes on the clock move faster and faster.

At 7:15 Juan parks his car, grabs his lunch, and runs to the entrance of the factory. He is very unhappy and very nervous.

Understanding New Words

(expanding vocabulary, using and understanding new words and phrases)

Read these sentences with a partner. Decide together if sentence *a* or *b* has the same meaning. Circle the sentence with the same meaning.

1. Juan is a little nervous and too excited to eat breakfast.

   a. Juan is sick.

   b. Juan thinks and worries about his new job.

2. Juan worries he will be late on his first day. He changes lanes.

   .. He stops his car and gets out.

   He moves his car to the right and to the left on the street.

3. He honks his horn at the cars in front of him.

   He makes a loud noise with his car horn.

   . He shouts at the cars in front of him.

4. He is angry about the traffic.

   He is angry about all the cars on the street.

   He is angry about the clock.

5. He starts to sweat. The minutes on the clock move faster and faster.

   He says some bad words.

   His face and hands become wet.

6. At 7:15 Juan parks his car, grabs his lunch, and runs to the entrance of the factory.

   He picks up his lunch quickly.

   . He eats his lunch.

Understanding the Reading

(checking literal and inferential comprehension)

Read these sentences with a partner. Decide together if they are true or false. Put a check (✔) in the column.

		True	False
1.	Today is Juan's first day on the job.	✔	
2.	The factory is seven miles from Juan's home.		
3.	Juan does not eat breakfast because he is sick.		
4.	Juan drinks coffee.		
5.	Juan's wife makes his lunch.		
6.	The clock in Juan's car does not work.		
7.	Juan is angry about all the traffic.		
8.	Juan walks slowly to the entrance of the factory.		
9.	Juan is unhappy and nervous when he gets to work on his first day.		

Discussing

Activity #1 *(completing a conversation, using critical thinking)*

Juan is late for work on his first day. With a partner, decide what Juan said to his boss. Write Juan's words on the lines.

BOSS: Are you Juan Lopez?

JUAN: ______________________________

BOSS: You're late.

JUAN: ______________________________

BOSS: Do you know what time we start?

JUAN: ______________________________

BOSS: What is your problem today?

JUAN: ______________________________

Activity #2 *(using creative thinking skills in role plays, empathizing with a character)*

1. Work with a partner. Partner A is the boss. The boss is angry when employees come late to work. The boss wants employees to come on time every day.

   Partner B is the employee. Today is the first time the employee is late to work in two years.
2. Partner B is the boss. The boss understands the problems employees have in the morning. The boss wants a late employee to work extra time.

   Partner A is the employee who is late every day for one week.

Activity #3 *(making judgments, using problem-solving skills, evaluating reasons for actions)*

With a partner read the reasons for being late for work. Decide together if the reason is a good reason or a bad reason. Put a check (✔) in the column. Talk about your answers with the class.

		Good reason	Bad reason
1.	The car breaks down.	______	______
2.	The babysitter does not come on time.	______	______
3.	The babysitter does not come.	______	______
4.	There is a traffic jam.	______	______
5.	You oversleep (sleep too late).	______	______
6.	You don't have a ride to work.	______	______
7.	You have a headache. (Your head hurts.)	______	______
8.	You forget your lunch. You go home to get it.	______	______
9.	You have a doctor's appointment.	______	______
10.	You have an accident with another car.	______	______
11.	You stop to buy a lottery ticket.	______	______
12.	You get a telephone call from your mother.	______	______

Reading at Work

Understanding New Words

(expanding vocabulary, using and understanding new words and phrases)

Read the sentences below. Find and circle the underlined words in the following reading.

1. Employees are workers in a factory, an office, or a hospital.
2. Juan and Carlota are 15 minutes late. They make up the time. They work an extra 15 minutes.
3. When employees skip breaks, they do not take breaks.
4. An employee receives less money when his pay is docked.
5. A terminated employee is fired and cannot work at the company.

Some companies have a policy about coming late to work. Read the company policy below.

Employees must arrive on time for work. Supervisors will check to see that all their employees are working at the correct start time. Employees who are late must make up the lost time. They may take a short lunch period, skip one or more breaks, or stay late to finish work. Employees who are late more than two times per week may have their pay docked. Employees who continue to arrive late for work may be terminated.

Understanding the Reading

(checking literal and inferential comprehension, relating reading to actual experiences)

A. Answer the questions. Write on the lines.

1. When must employees arrive for work? ____________________
2. What must late employees do? ____________________
3. What happens to employees who are late three times in one week? ____________________
4. Can employees be terminated for arriving late many times? ____________________

B. Work with a small group of three or four people. Talk about what happens when people are late to work at your company. Answer the questions.

1. Are you ever late for work? Why?
2. How do you feel when you are late?
3. What happens to you if you are late?

Writing

(constructing sentences, using present-tense verbs, using frequency adverbs)

Make sentences with the words below. Write the sentences on the lines.

I My friend My boss Some friends The employees	am is are	always usually sometimes never	late for work early for work	on Mondays. one day a month. when the bus is late. when they drive. when there is a traffic jam.

1. I am sometimes late for work on Mondays.
2. ____________________
3. ____________________
4. ____________________
5. ____________________

Listening

Activity #1 *(listening for specific information)*

Listen to the tape of the conversations. Circle the correct picture.

Activity #2 *(listening for specific information, completing sentences, understanding context clues)*

Listen to the traffic report on the tape. Use the words in the box to complete the report.

heavy	990	Main Street	morning	traffic
downtown	north	River Road	over	20

Well, here's the ____________ traffic from station WESL, number ____________ on your AM dial. The ____________ looks good from School Street to ____________ ____________. Becoming ____________ around the Wilson Bridge. It'll take you ____________ minutes to go from the Wilson Bridge into ____________ Rockford. There's construction on the ____________ side of Harding Road, so watch out for it. A better altenative would be ____________ exit to Route 17, then ____________ to Harding Road. That's it for Central Traffic Control.

Activity # 3 *(listening to traffic reports, discussing problems)*

Listen to the traffic report on your radio. Where is the traffic heavy? Do you have to change the way you drive to work? Is there construction on the streets you take to get to work? What do you do when there is construction on the streets you take to get to work? Talk with a partner about the problems of traffic jams.

Reading Charts and Using Math

(reading charts, using information to complete a chart, subtracting whole numbers)

In/Out Time

The work day starts at 7:00 a.m. and ends at 3:30 p.m. Read the chart with a partner.

Day	Monday 6/18		Tuesday 6/19		Wednesday 6/20		Thursday 6/21		Friday 6/22	
Name	in	out	in	out	in	out	in	out	in	out
M. Porter	6:50	3:31	6:55	3:30	6:57	3:29	7:03	4:32	7:00	3:30
J. Gomez	6:45	3:40	7:15	3:50	6:50	3:30	6:55	3:29	6:47	3:30
K. Bys	7:01	3:30	7:05	3:29	7:00	3:28	7:08	3:29	7:02	3:31
S. Lee	7:06	3:33	7:00	3:31	7:10	3:30	7:00	3:30	7:12	3:31
K. Park	7:02	3:39	6:53	3:30	6:55	3:31	6:57	3:30	6:59	3:30
E. Rodriguez	6:49	3:30	6:53	3:30	6:58	3:30	6:55	3:30	6:54	3:30

Work with a partner. Complete the chart below. Write the number of minutes each employee is late to work each day.

	Mon. 6/18	Tues. 6/19	Wed. 6/20	Thurs. 6/21	Fri. 6/22	Total number of minutes late per week
M. Porter	0	0	0	3	0	3 minutes
J. Gomez	0	15	0	0	0	15 minutes
K. Bys						
S. Lee						
K. Park						
E. Rodriguez						

1. Who is on time most often?______________________

2. Who is late most often?______________________

UNIT 2 *Giving/Following Directions and Instructions*

Before You Read

(making predictions, relating experiences to reading, establishing prior knowledge)

Hakim Raquib

Look at the picture.

Talk about this picture with a partner.

Read the questions.

Write your answers on the lines.

1. Where are these people? in a restaurant
2. What are the people doing? seHing the table
3. What food can you eat in this restaurant? oreilatal
4. When do you go to a restaurant? ______
5. What food do you like to eat in a restaurant? ______

Reading About Work

Kim and the Golden Dragon

Kim is on a bus. She is going to the Golden Dragon Restaurant where she works. Today is Kim's second day of work. She is thinking about the instructions from her boss. Kim is a little nervous. She is afraid that she will not remember all the instructions. Kim talks quietly to herself on the bus.

"First, I say 'Hello' to the customers and tell my name. Then I ask if they want drinks. I write down the drink orders and serve them. After I serve the drinks, I write down the food orders. If customers want a salad, I ask what kind of salad dressing they want. If customers want steaks, I ask if they like the steaks rare, medium, or well done. I ask if they want french fries, baked potatoes, mashed potatoes, or rice. After I serve the food, I see if the customers want more drinks.

"When they finish eating, I ask if they want to order dessert. After I serve dessert and coffee or tea, I give them the check for their food and drinks. I say 'Thank you' and tell them to pay the cashier near the front door."

As Kim finishes thinking about the instructions, the bus stops in front of the Golden Dragon Restaurant. Kim does not look nervous, but her hands are shaking as she opens the door and goes inside.

Understanding New Words

(expanding vocabulary, understanding and using new words)

Read these sentences with a partner. Decide together if *a* or *b* has the same meaning. Circle *a* or *b*.

1. Kim is thinking about the instructions from her boss.

   a. the directions to be a waitress
   b. the names of the food and drinks

2. I say "Hello" to the customers and tell my name.

   a. the other workers and my boss
   b. the people who pay for the food in the restaurant

3. After I serve the drinks, I write down the food orders.

   a. bring the drinks to the table and put them in front of the customers
   b. tell the names of the drinks

4. I ask if the customers want to order dessert.

   a. cake, ice cream, or pie
   b. a sandy place in Africa

5. I give the customers the check for their food and drinks.
   a. the menu with the foods the restaurant makes
   b. a paper with the prices for the food and drink orders

6. I tell them to pay the cashier near the front door.
   a. the person who takes the money for the food and drinks
   b. the pretty woman at the table near the door

Understanding the Reading

(checking literal and inferential comprehension)

Read these sentences with a partner. Decide together if they are true or false. Put a check (✔) in the column.

		True	False
1.	Kim takes a bus to go to work.	____	____
2.	Today is Kim's first day at work.	____	____
3.	Kim talks to herself on the way to work.	____	____
4.	Kim writes down the drink orders and serves them.	____	____
5.	Kim gives every customer a salad.	____	____
6.	Customers order steaks rare, medium, or well done.	____	____
7.	The Golden Dragon Restaurant only makes french fries.	____	____
8.	Customers order dessert before they eat dinner.	____	____
9.	Customers pay the waitress for their dinner.	____	____
10.	Kim is nervous as she goes inside the restaurant.	____	____

Discussing

Activity #1 *(completing a conversation, using critical thinking skills)*

Kim's first customer is Mr. Fuller. He eats dinner at the Golden Dragon Restaurant about four times every week. With a partner, decide what Mr. Fuller wants to eat today. Write his words on the lines.

Here are some foods that the restaurant serves:

salads: with French dressing, Italian dressing, or Bleu Cheese dressing

main dishes: sweet and sour pork baked chicken with pineapple steak shrimp

side dishes: baked potato mashed potato french fries rice

vegetables: green beans carrots peas corn

desserts: apple pie cherry pie chocolate cake fortune cookies

drinks: coffee tea milk Coke® 7-Up® orange juice

KIM: Hello. My name is Kim. Do you want something to drink?

MR. FULLER: Yes I would like ~~coffee~~ tea

KIM: Here is your tea. Are you ready to order your dinner?

MR. FULLER: Yes, I would like steak

KIM: Your dinner comes with a salad. What kind of salad dressing do you want?

MR. FULLER: Italian

KIM: What side dish and vegetable do you want?

MR. FULLER: baked potatoe and corn

I don't think I will have any dessert tonight. Thank you, young lady.

Activity #2 *(using creative thinking skills in role plays, empathizing with a character)*

1. Work with a group of three students. Student A is the waiter or waitress at the Golden Dragon Restaurant. Students B and C are friends. Student B is very hungry and wants to order dinner. Student C is not very hungry and only wants to order dessert.
2. Student B is the waiter or waitress. Student A wants to order apple pie before ordering dinner. Student C wants to order dinner but does not want salad dressing or a vegetable with the dinner.

Activity #3 *(making judgments about polite and impolite statements, using critical thinking skills)*

Some people say polite things in a restaurant. Some people say impolite things in a restaurant.

Examples: Polite—"Thank you. Enjoy your dinner."

Impolite—"Get me some more salad dressing this minute."

Read the sentences with a partner. Decide together if the words are *polite* or *impolite*. Circle *polite* or *impolite*. Talk about your answers with the class.

1. "I want chocolate milk. I will not drink this white milk!" **polite impolite**
2. "May I bring you more coffee?" **polite impolite**
3. "Where is that waiter? I'm hungry." **polite impolite**
4. "No, thank you. I do not want any dessert." **polite impolite**
5. "I want my steak well done. This is rare. Take it back and cook it right this time." **polite impolite**
6. "I'm sorry, but I didn't order chicken. I ordered shrimp." **polite impolite**

Reading at Work

Understanding New Words

(expanding vocabulary, understanding and using words in context)

Read the sentences below. Find and circle the underlined words in the following reading.

1. The Johnson family likes Chinese food. They frequently eat at the Golden Dragon Restaurant. They eat there three or four times every week.
2. Kim always tries to be polite and friendly to her customers. She is courteous when she speaks to them and serves them.
3. Please write legibly on your application. Then another person can read and understand your application.
4. Appetizers are foods that you eat before your lunch or dinner.
5. ASAP means "as soon as possible." Give the food order to the cook ASAP.

Some restaurants have reminders (things to remember) for their workers. Read the reminders for servers below.

Reminders for Servers

Remember to
1. check your work schedule for days, hours, and table assignments.
2. wash your hands frequently while working.
3. be friendly and courteous to all customers.
4. write legibly on your order tickets.
5. serve drinks and appetizers ASAP.
6. refill salt, pepper, and sugar containers when you are not busy with customers.

Understanding the Reading

(checking literal and inferential comprehension, relating reading to actual experiences)

A. Answer the questions. Write on the lines.

1. Why do the servers check the schedule? ______________________
2. Why do the servers write legibly on the order tickets? ______________________

____

3. Why is it important for servers to wash their hands frequently? __________

____

4. Why do the servers serve the drinks and appetizers ASAP? ______________

____

B. Work with a small group of three or four people. Talk about your job and your workplace. Answer the questions.

1. What does a courteous employee do? What does a courteous employee say to other people?
2. What must you do ASAP on your job?
3. When is it important for you to write legibly?

Writing

(constructing sentences with imperatives, sequencing and prioritizing information)

Write a list of reminders for your job.

Reminders for (name of job) ____________________

Remember to

1. ____
2. ____
3. ____
4. ____

Listening

Activity #1 *(listening for specific information, ordering food in a restaurant)*

Listen to the tape of the people in a restaurant. Circle the words to show what each person orders.

Customer ***A*** orders: salad with French dressing Italian dressing
Bleu Cheese dressing no dressing
sweet and sour pork baked chicken steak shrimp
apple pie cherry pie chocolate cake fortune cookies
coffee tea orange juice tomato juice Coke® Pepsi® milk

Customer ***B*** orders: salad with French dressing Italian dressing
Bleu Cheese dressing no dressing
sweet and sour pork baked chicken steak shrimp
apple pie cherry pie chocolate cake fortune cookies
coffee tea orange juice tomato juice Coke® Pepsi® milk

Customer ***C*** orders: salad with French dressing Italian dressing
Bleu Cheese dressing no dressing
sweet and sour pork baked chicken steak shrimp
apple pie cherry pie chocolate cake fortune cookies
coffee tea orange juice tomato juice Coke® Pepsi® milk

Activity #2 *(identifying the speaker from context clues)*

Listen to the tape. Circle the picture to show who is talking.

1.

2.

3.

Using Math

(adding decimals, calculating percents)

Here is a check for one customer at the Golden Dragon Restaurant. Add the prices and write the subtotal on the check.

To figure the tax, you multiply the subtotal by .05, which is 5%.

Step 1: Multiply $13.50

x .05

6750

Step 2: Count the number of decimal places in both numbers you multiply. Add them.

$13.50	2 decimal places
x .05	+ 2 decimal places
.6750	4 decimal places

Step 3: Count 4 decimal places in the answer.

$13.50

x .05

.6750 The tax is .67 (67 cents) or .68 (68 cents). Write the tax on the check.

Step 4: Add the tax to the subtotal. Write the total on the check.

$13.50

\+ .67

$14.17

GUEST CHECK				
TABLE NO. 1	NO. PERSONS 1	CHECK NO. 905	SERVER Kim	
1	Chicken Noodle Soup	1	.50	
1	Sweet + sour pork	10	.50	
	salad - Bleu cheese rice			
	peas coffee			
1	Cherry pie	1	.50	
	subtotal			
	5% tax			
	total			
	15% tip			

To figure the tip, multiply the total by .15, which is 15%.

$14.17	2 decimal places
x .15	+ 2 decimal places
7085	4 decimal places
+ 1417	
2.1255	The tip is $2.12 or $2.13. Write the tip on the check.

How much did the customer at Table 1 pay for the food and the tip? ____________

Look at these checks for Tables 2, 3, 4, and 5.

1. Add the prices and write the subtotals.
2. Figure the 5% tax.
3. Add the tax to the subtotal and write the total.
4. Figure the 15% tip.
5. How much did Kim receive in tips from the checks on this page? ________

GUEST CHECK

TABLE NO.	NO. PERSONS	CHECK NO.	SERVER
2	1	906	Kim

1	Sirloin Steak	12	.75
	salad - French		
	FF		
	corn		
	milk		
1	Choc. cake	2	.00
	subtotal		
	5% tax		
	Total		
	15% tip		

GUEST CHECK

TABLE NO.	NO. PERSONS	CHECK NO.	SERVER
3	2	907	Kim

1	Veg. soup	1	.50
1	Salad - Italian	2	.00
1	Tea		.50
1	Apple Pie	1	.50
1	salad - Italian	2	.00
1	Fortune cookies	1	.25
1	7-up		.75
	subtotal		
	5% tax		
	Total		
	15% tip		

GUEST CHECK

TABLE NO.	NO. PERSONS	CHECK NO.	SERVER
4	1	908	Kim

1	Shrimp	11	.25
	salad - French rice		
	green beans		
1	Coke		.75
1	Fortune Cookies	1	.25
	subtotal		.
	5% tax		.
	Total		.
	15% tip		.

GUEST CHECK

TABLE NO.	NO. PERSONS	CHECK NO.	SERVER
5	2	909	Kim

1	Baked Chicken	10	.25
	mashed peas		
	coffee		
1	Sirloin Steak	12	.75
	salad - Bleu Cheese baked		
	carrots milk		
1	Choc Cake	2	.00
	subtotal		.
	5% tax		.
	Total		.
	15% tip		.

"Say, this isn't 35th and Main."

UNIT 3 *Safety*

Before You Read
(making predictions, relating experiences to reading, establishing prior knowledge)

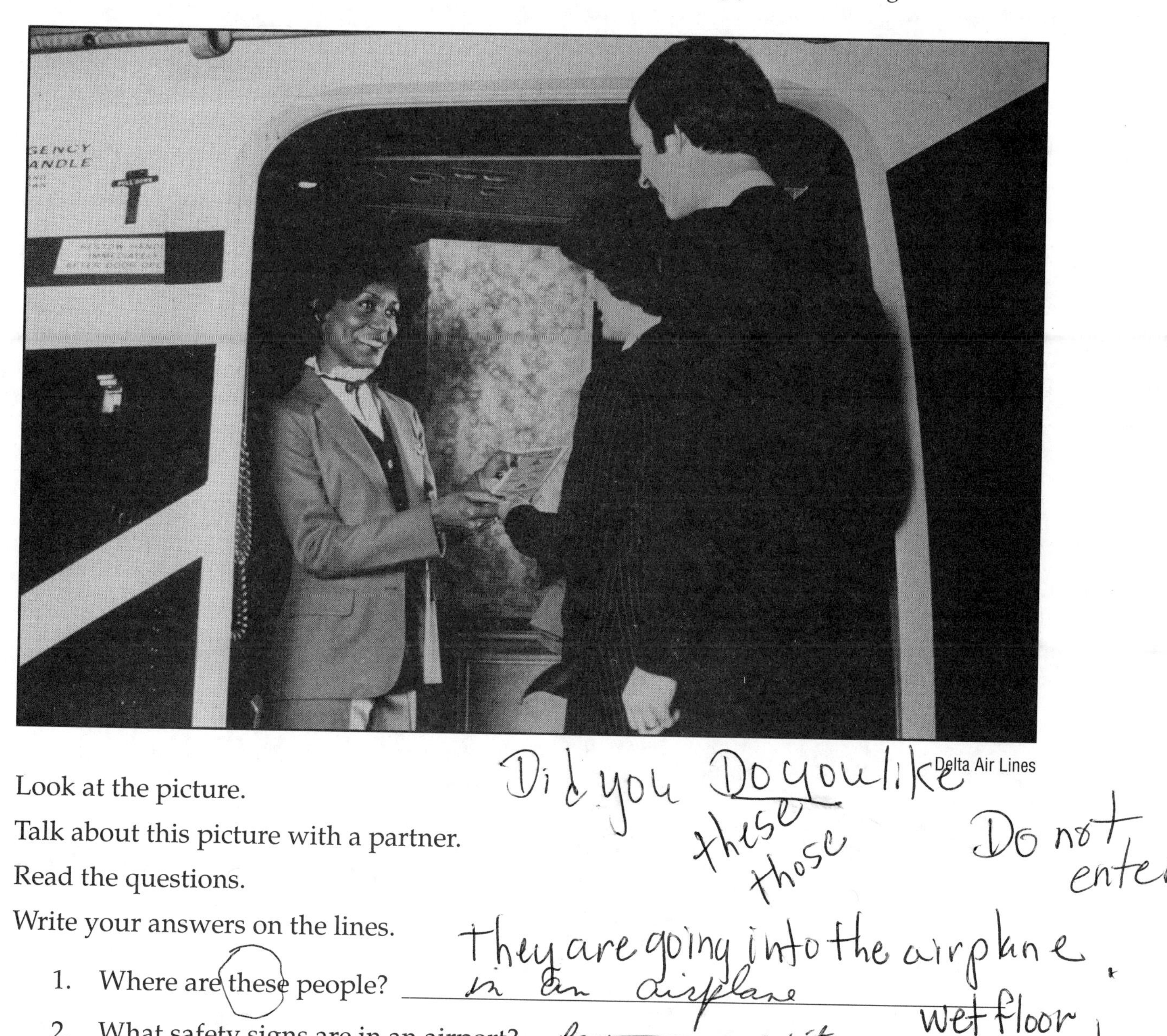

Delta Air Lines

Look at the picture.
Talk about this picture with a partner.
Read the questions.
Write your answers on the lines.

1. Where are these people? ______________________________
2. What safety signs are in an airport? ______________________________
3. Do you sometimes fly in an airplane? ______________________________
4. Do you like to fly in an airplane? __________ Why or why not? __________
____

Reading About Work

Sylvia's Safe Skies

(Sylvia and Monica meet at the airport.)

MONICA: Hi, Sylvia! What a surprise to see you here!

SYLVIA: Hi, Monica. I work here now. I have a new job. I'm a flight attendant.

MONICA: That's great. Do you like your new job as a flight attendant?

SYLVIA: I like it a lot. I learn new things every day. I have a lot of responsibility, too.

MONICA: What kind of responsibility?

SYLVIA: Well, I'm responsible for every passenger's safety. Part of my job is helping passengers arrive safely at their destinations. I explain all the safety procedures before the airplane leaves the ground.

MONICA: What safety procedures?

SYLVIA: I tell all the passengers to put on their seat belts during takeoff and landing and also when the "Fasten Seat Belt" sign is on. I tell passengers there is no smoking on the airplane. I show where the emergency exits are. Then I explain how to use the emergency exits to leave the airplane. I also show how to use an oxygen mask.

MONICA: An oxygen mask? Do your passengers need oxygen masks?

SYLVIA: Most passengers don't. But one passenger with heart trouble needed some oxygen. He's afraid of flying. The next time he goes to see his grandchildren, he will take the train.

MONICA: That sounds like my grandfather. In fact, that's why I'm here—to pick up my grandfather. There he is.

SYLVIA: Oh, no. Your grandfather is the passenger I am talking about!

Understanding New Words

(expanding vocabulary, using new words and phrases)

A. Work with a partner. Read the words in the box. Find the words in the story on page 22. Circle the words.

flight attendant	responsible	passengers	oxygen mask	destination

B. Finish the sentence. Write words from the box on the line. Read the sentences with your partner.

1. You have trouble breathing. You need an oxygen mask to help you.
2. My car has room for five passengers, or riders.
3. Sylvia is responsible for the safety of the passengers.
4. The place you are going to is your destination.
5. A flight attendant helps passengers find their seats in an airplane and serves the food and drinks.

C. Cross out the word or phrase that does not belong.

1. passengers riders ~~flight attendant~~
2. ~~afraid~~ oxygen air
3. airport ~~train~~ ~~restaurant~~
4. tell explain ~~fasten~~
5. exit door ~~grandfather~~
6. place to go ~~emergency~~ destination

It is your responsibility

"Flight attendant"

Flight

I missed my Flight.

Do you catch your Flight?

Do you go on the airplane

Understanding the Reading

(checking literal and inferential comprehension)

Work with your partner. Match the words in *Part A* and *Part B* to make sentences. Write the sentences on the lines.

Part A	Part B
1. Sylvia likes her job	a lot of responsibility.
2. Sylvia and Monica	about safety procedures.
3. A flight attendant has	the seat belt during takeoff and landing.
4. The flight attendant tells the passengers	as a flight attendant.
5. One safety procedure is to put on	are friends.
6. Another safety procedure is to know	needed an oxygen mask.
7. Monica's grandfather	where the emergency exits are.

1. Sylvia likes her job as a flight attendant.

2. ____________________

3. ____________________

4. ____________________

5. ____________________

6. ____________________

7. ____________________

Discussing

Activity #1 *(identifying unsafe working conditions, suggesting solutions to safety problems)*

Here is the kitchen of an airport restaurant. Look at the picture. What safety problems do you see? Circle the problems. Talk with your partner. What can you do to make this a safe place to work?

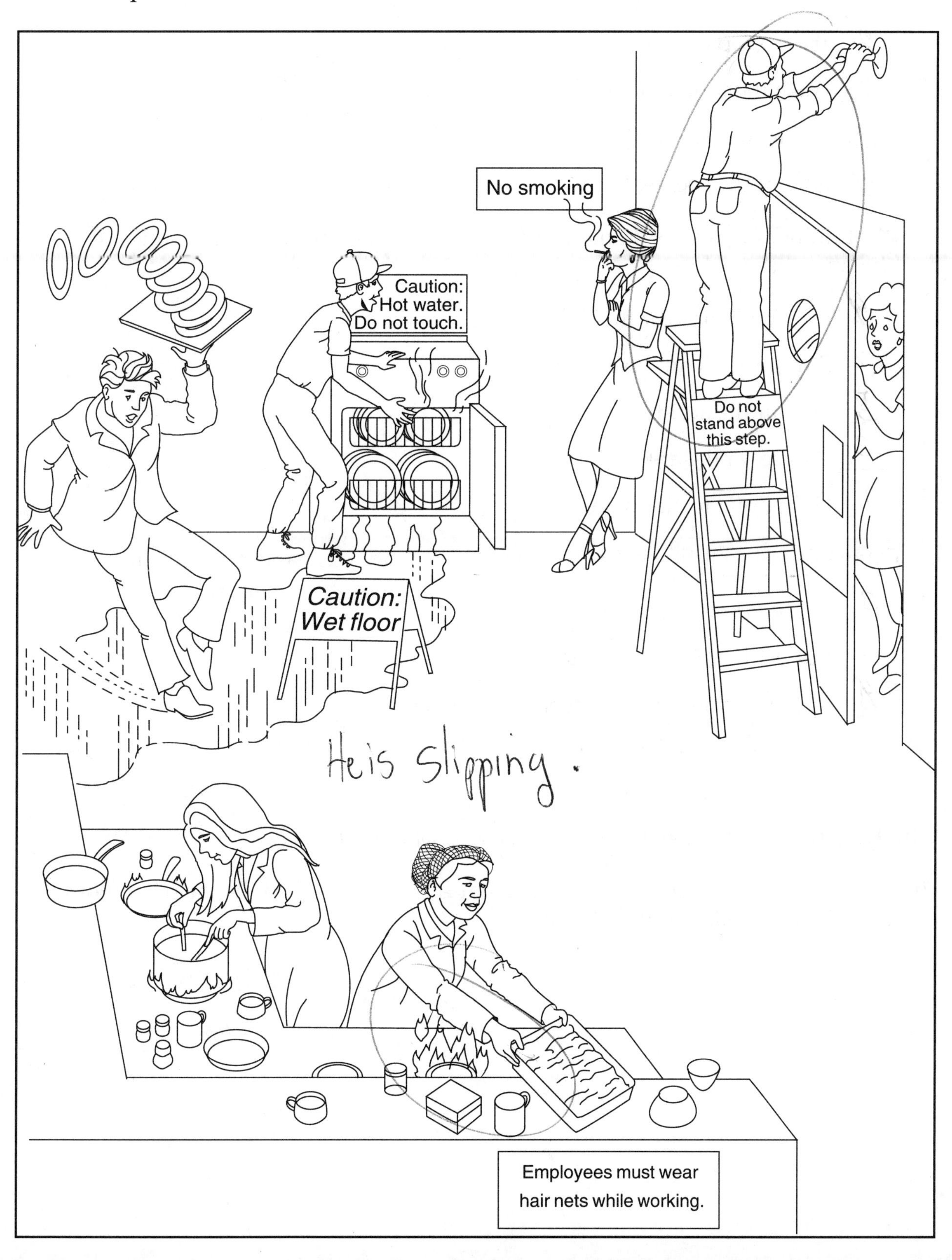

2.02

Activity #2 *(using problem-solving skills, sequencing events in an emergency)*

Read about three accidents. Write 1 before the first thing to do. Write 2 before the second thing to do, and so on. Check your answers with your partner.

1. Rodolfo cut his toe on a sharp nail in the floor at the factory. The cut is deep.

   ______ Go to see the doctor or nurse if the cut is deep.

   ______ Try to stop the bleeding.

   __1__ Wash the foot and toe.

   ______ Fix the nail in the floor.

   ______ Fill out the accident report.

2. It is raining. Zofia slips on the wet floor near the door of her office building. She hurts her ankle.

   ______ Dry the floor near the door.

   ______ Put the ankle up on a chair or desk.

   ______ Fill out the accident report.

   ______ Put ice on the ankle.

   ______ Help Zofia to sit down.

3. On break, Joe spills hot coffee and burns his hand. His hand is very red.

   ______ Fill out the accident report.

   ______ Put the hand in cold water.

   ______ Put medicine from the doctor on the hand.

   ______ Go to see a doctor or nurse.

Activity #3 *(using creative thinking skills in a role play, empathizing with a character)*

Student A is Joe in accident #3 above. Student B is the boss. Joe tells the boss about his accident. The boss tells Joe what to do.

Reading at Work

2.01

Understanding New Words

(expanding vocabulary, using new words and phrases)

Read the sentences below. Find and circle the underlined words in the following safety signs.

1. Caution means to be careful. Use caution when driving in the rain.
2. I reduce the speed I drive from 40 MPH to 30 MPH.
3. The maximum capacity is the largest number of people who can fit safely in one place. The restaurant has a maximum capacity of 60 people.
4. Paint is flammable. It can start on fire.
5. The balloon is up high in a tree. It is out of reach of the little girl.

Read these safety signs and labels. Draw a line from the sign or label to the place you see it.

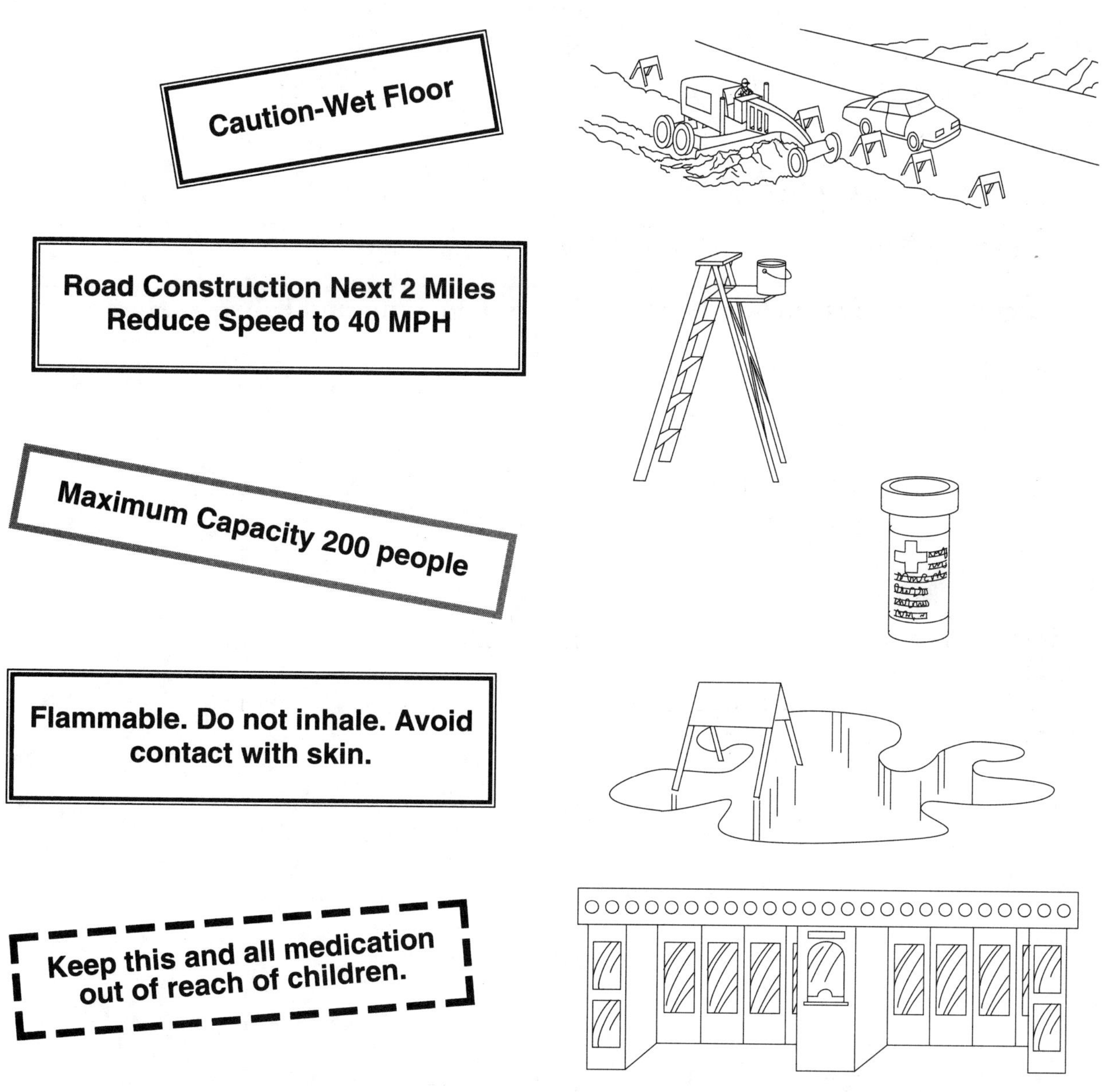

Understanding the Reading

(using vocabulary in context, identifying and reading safety signs and labels, making inferences)

A. Write the words on the lines.

1. Use ______________________ when you walk on a wet floor.
2. A big truck carries __________________ gasoline.
3. Our school is small. The ____________ ____________ is 100 people.

B. Work with a small group of three or four people. Talk about the safety signs you see at work. Answer the questions.

1. Where do you see safety signs?
2. What do the signs say?
3. What other safety signs do you need at work?
4. Where do you see safety labels at home?
5. What do the labels say?

Writing

(identifying and writing safety signs and labels, understanding and using imperatives)

Look for safety signs and labels. Write the words on the lines.

Safety Signs and Labels at Work	Safety Signs and Labels at Home
______________________________	______________________________
______________________________	______________________________
______________________________	______________________________
______________________________	______________________________
______________________________	______________________________

Listening

Activity #1 *(listening for specific information, using auditory discrimination)*

Listen to the tape of the flight attendant. Circle the words you hear.

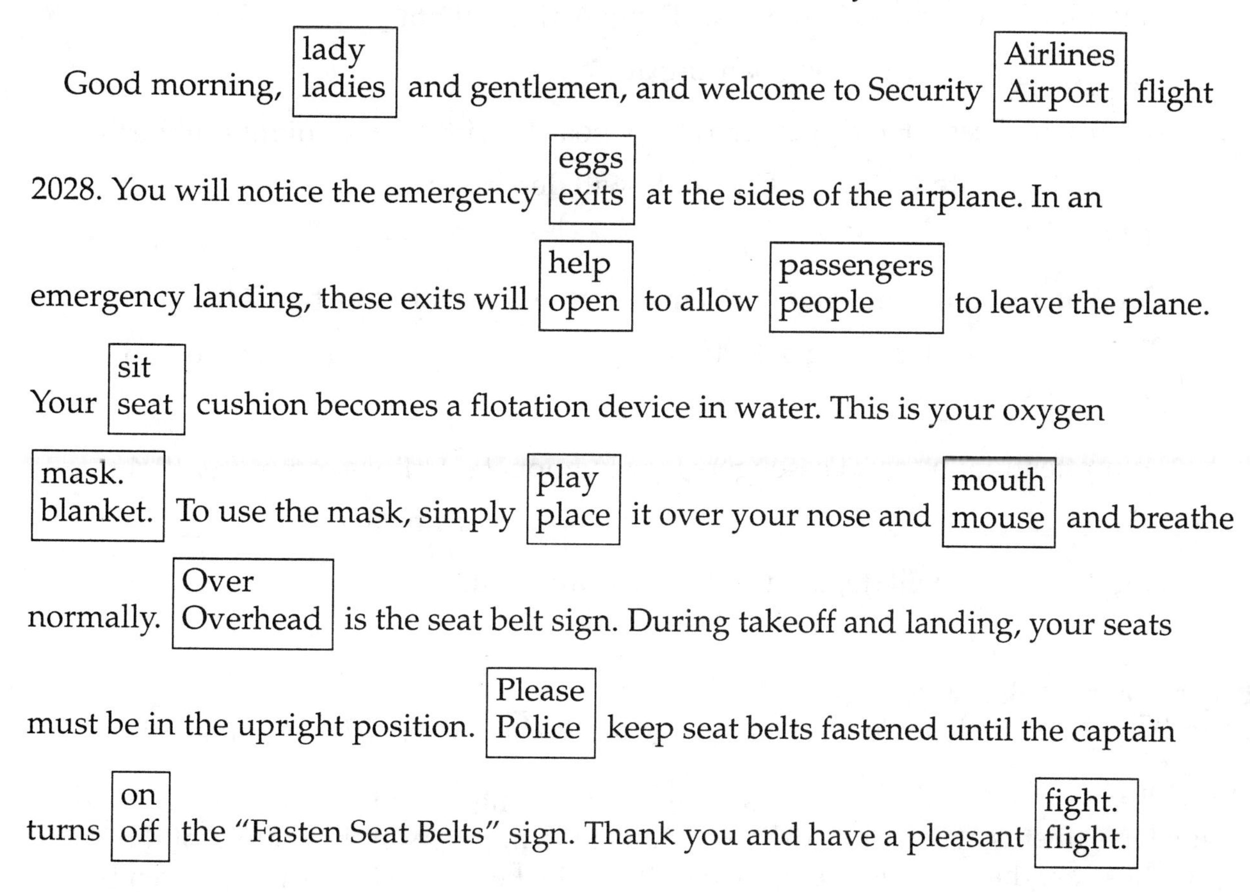

Good morning, [lady / ladies] and gentlemen, and welcome to Security [Airlines / Airport] flight 2028. You will notice the emergency [eggs / exits] at the sides of the airplane. In an emergency landing, these exits will [help / open] to allow [passengers / people] to leave the plane. Your [sit / seat] cushion becomes a flotation device in water. This is your oxygen [mask. / blanket.] To use the mask, simply [play / place] it over your nose and [mouth / mouse] and breathe normally. [Over / Overhead] is the seat belt sign. During takeoff and landing, your seats must be in the upright position. [Please / Police] keep seat belts fastened until the captain turns [on / off] the "Fasten Seat Belts" sign. Thank you and have a pleasant [fight. / flight.]

Activity #2 *(listening for specific numbers, letters, and names)*

Listen to the tape. Write the flight number, the gate number, and the destination.

1. May I have your attention, please. Eagle Airlines flight ________ for ________________ is now boarding at Gate ________.
2. Attention, please. Passengers may now board Swift Airlines flight number ________ at Gate ________. This flight will depart for ________________ at 12:19 P.M.
3. Good afternoon, ladies and gentlemen. Passengers for Sky High Airlines flight ________, departing at 2:30 for ________________, may now board at Gate ________.
4. Your attention, please. Passengers for Skyhoppers Airlines commuter flight ________ to ____________________ are now boarding at Gate ________. Flight ________ will depart at 3:45 P.M. Thank you.

Using Math and a Bar Graph

(interpreting a bar graph, adding and subtracting whole numbers, figuring percentages)

This is a bar graph. Read the title. Read the words on the left side of the graph. These are the departments at Security Airlines. Look at the numbers at the bottom of the graph. These are the number of employees. Read the key. The key shows how many employees are men and how many are women.

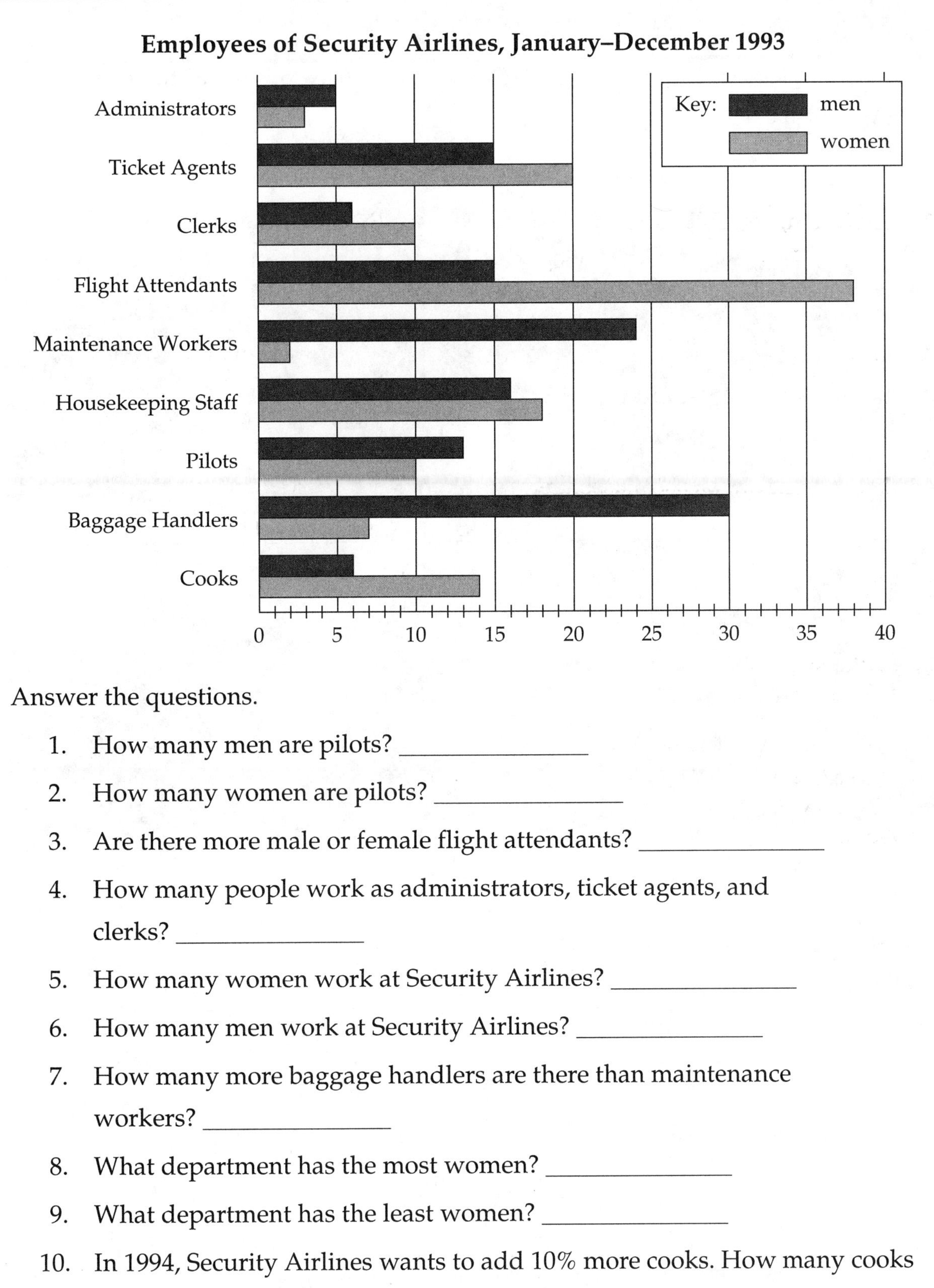

Answer the questions.

1. How many men are pilots? _______________
2. How many women are pilots? _______________
3. Are there more male or female flight attendants? _______________
4. How many people work as administrators, ticket agents, and clerks? _______________
5. How many women work at Security Airlines? _______________
6. How many men work at Security Airlines? _______________
7. How many more baggage handlers are there than maintenance workers? _______________
8. What department has the most women? _______________
9. What department has the least women? _______________
10. In 1994, Security Airlines wants to add 10% more cooks. How many cooks will work at the airlines in 1994? _______________
11. In 1994, Security Airlines wants to add 15% more workers to the housekeeping staff. How many people will work in housekeeping in 1994? _______________

UNIT 4 *Interacting with Co-workers*

Before You Read

(making predictions, relating experiences to reading, establishing prior knowledge)

Courtesy McDonald Corp.
Joseph Nettis/Photo Researchers
Bill Losh/FPG International

Look at the pictures.

Talk about the pictures with a partner.

Read the questions.

Write the answers on the lines.

1. What are all the people in the pictures doing? ____________________
2. Where are the people in picture 1? ____________________

   In picture 2? ____________________ In picture 3? ____________________

   In picture 4? ____________________
3. What do you think the people in picture 1 are talking about?

   In picture 2? ____________________

   In picture 3? ____________________

   In picture 4? ____________________

Reading About Work

Small Talk at Freddy's Finest Foods

(It is lunch time at Freddy's Finest Foods. Some of the employees are eating lunch in the lunchroom. Stanley is sitting alone at one table. Lillian and Raymond come to the table.)

RAYMOND: Hi, Stanley. May we join you?

STANLEY: Sure.

RAYMOND: Thanks. This is Lillian Walkowski. She's new in town. She works as a cashier here. Lillian, this is Stanley Johnson.

STANLEY: Hello, Lillian. It's nice to meet you. Please sit down.

LILLIAN: Thanks, my feet are killing me.

STANLEY: I remember my first week here. My feet hurt all the time. Forty hours is a long time to stand on your feet. I'm always glad when Friday comes.

RAYMOND: Speaking of Friday, what are you doing this weekend?

STANLEY: I'm going to study all weekend. I have a big test coming up in my computer class on Monday night. I want to be ready. I also want to sleep late on Saturday morning. I'm up almost every night with my new baby. What are you going to do, Raymond?

RAYMOND: Today is payday, so I have a little money to spend. I think I'll take my girlfriend to a movie tonight and maybe we'll go dancing on Saturday. My girlfriend loves to dance, but I have two left feet. Do you have plans for the weekend, Lillian?

LILLIAN: I still have boxes to unpack in my apartment. On Sunday I'll go grocery shopping with my cousin.

STANLEY: Where do you go grocery shopping?

LILLIAN: Any store but Freddy's Finest Foods. I like my job, but this is one place I don't want to be on my day off.

Understanding New Words

(expanding and using new words and phrases)

A. Work with a partner. Read the words in the box. Find the words in the story on page 33. Circle the words.

payday	day off	are killing me	I'm up	have two left feet

B. Read the sentences. Circle *a*, *b*, or *c*.

1. I can't dance very well. I have two left feet. This means
   a. dancing is very difficult for me.
   b. I wear two left shoes.
   c. I can dance only with my left foot.
2. When I say my feet are killing me, I mean
   a. my feet hurt.
   b. my toes kill other toes.
   c. I do not like my feet.
3. Friday is payday at my company. Payday is
   a. the day I do not have any money.
   b. the day workers pay their bosses.
   c. the day the workers get their money for working.
4. Luis likes to go to a baseball game on Saturday, his day off. A day off is
   a. a day when you do only a little work.
   b. a day you do not go to work.
   c. a bad day.
5. Stanley says, "I'm up almost every night with my new baby." Stanley means
   a. he is awake and not sleeping part of the night.
   b. he is up on the roof at night.
   c. he has trouble sleeping, so he watches television.

Understanding the Reading

(checking literal and inferential comprehension)

A. Work with your partner. Match the words in Part A and Part B to make sentences. Write the sentences on the lines.

Part A	Part B
1. Stanley is sitting	are killing her.
2. Stanley wants Raymond and Lillian	when Friday comes.
3. Lillian's feet	alone at one table in the lunchroom.
4. Stanley is always glad	to join him at his table.

1. ______________________________

2. ______________________________

____

3. ______________________________

4. ______________________________

B. Answer the questions. Write on the lines.

1. Why are Lillian's feet killing her? ______________________________

____

2. Why is Stanley so tired? ______________________________

____

3. Why does Raymond like payday?______________________________

____

4. Why does Lillian still have boxes to unpack in her apartment? ______________

____

Discussing

Activity #1 *(judging appropriate and inappropriate topics, using critical thinking skills)*

Some questions are *appropriate* to ask co-workers. For example, you can ask, "Where do you live?" or "When did you start working here?" Some things are *not appropriate* to ask co-workers. They may be too personal. Co-workers do not talk about very personal things. For example, it is *inappropriate* to ask, "How much do you weigh?" "How much money do you make?" or "Why don't you have any children?"

A. Work with a partner. Read the questions. Decide together if they are appropriate or inappropriate to ask a co-worker. Circle *appropriate* or *inappropriate.* Talk about your answers with the class.

1. I like your haircut. Where do you get your hair cut?	*appropriate*	*inappropriate*
2. Do you live near your job?	*appropriate*	*inappropriate*
3. Do you have a boyfriend or girlfriend?	*appropriate*	*inappropriate*
4. Your feet look big. What size shoes do you wear?	*appropriate*	*inappropriate*
5. I understand you have a new house. How much did you pay for it?	*appropriate*	*inappropriate*
6. How did you and your husband or wife meet?	*appropriate*	*inappropriate*
7. Do you feel well today?	*appropriate*	*inappropriate*
8. Why are you divorced from your husband or wife?	*appropriate*	*inappropriate*
9. Can you show me how to work this machine?	*appropriate*	*inappropriate*
10. Your baby is four years old. When are you going to have another baby?	*appropriate*	*inappropriate*
11. What do you like to do on your day off?	*appropriate*	*inappropriate*
12. Why don't you have money for a new car?	*appropriate*	*inappropriate*

B. Write appropriate questions these people can ask you.

1. your best friend ____________________

2. a co-worker ____________________

3. a person in your family ____________________

4. your boss ____________________

Activity #2 *(using creative thinking skills in role plays, empathizing with a character)*

Work with a small group of three or four students.

1. Student A is a new employee at your company. Students B, C, and D are eating lunch in the company lunchroom. Student A sits alone at a table to eat. He or she does not know any of the employees. Students B, C, and D are friendly. They invite Student A to eat lunch with them. They ask Student A appropriate questions.
2. Student B is a new employee. He or she has a lunch from home to eat. He or she does not have much money. Students A, C, and D invite Student B to go out to a restaurant for lunch. They agree to pay for the new employee's lunch.
3. Employees have 45 minutes for lunch. Student C is a new employee. He or she is eating lunch with Students A, B, and D. After 45 minutes, the new employee wants to go back to work, but the other employees are not ready to go back.
4. It is break time. Students A, B, C, and D are sitting at one table in the lunchroom. Student D is a new employee. Students A, B, and C are complaining about their boss. They do not like the boss. They ask Student D what he or she thinks about the boss.

Reading at Work

Understanding New Words and Abbreviations

(expanding vocabulary, using new vocabulary and abbreviations)

A. Read the sentences below. Find and circle the underlined words and abbreviations in the bulletin-board messages on page 38.

1. My car is an '88 Pontiac. The manufacturer is Pontiac. The year is 1988.
2. This car has a V8 engine. There are 8 cylinders. Some cars have 4 or 6 cylinders.
3. The sign says "Chicago 66 mi." This means Chicago is 66 miles away.
4. My car runs very well. It looks great. It is in mint condition. I am asking $9,000. If you offer $8,750, I will take it.
5. When you write obo you mean "or best offer."

B. Match the abbreviations with the words. Find and circle the abbreviations in the bulletin-board messages on this page.

Abbreviations	Words
1. _____ apt.	A. Avenue
2. _____ vic.	B. bedroom
3. _____ Ave.	C. electricity
4. _____ rm	D. Department
5. _____ BR	E. vicinity (near)
6. _____ elec.	F. October 1st
7. _____ incl.	G. rooms
8. _____ avail.	H. included
9. _____ 10/1	I. available
10. _____ Dept.	J. apartment

Some companies have an employee bulletin board. This is a place to put messages for other employees to read. Read the messages on this employee bulletin board.

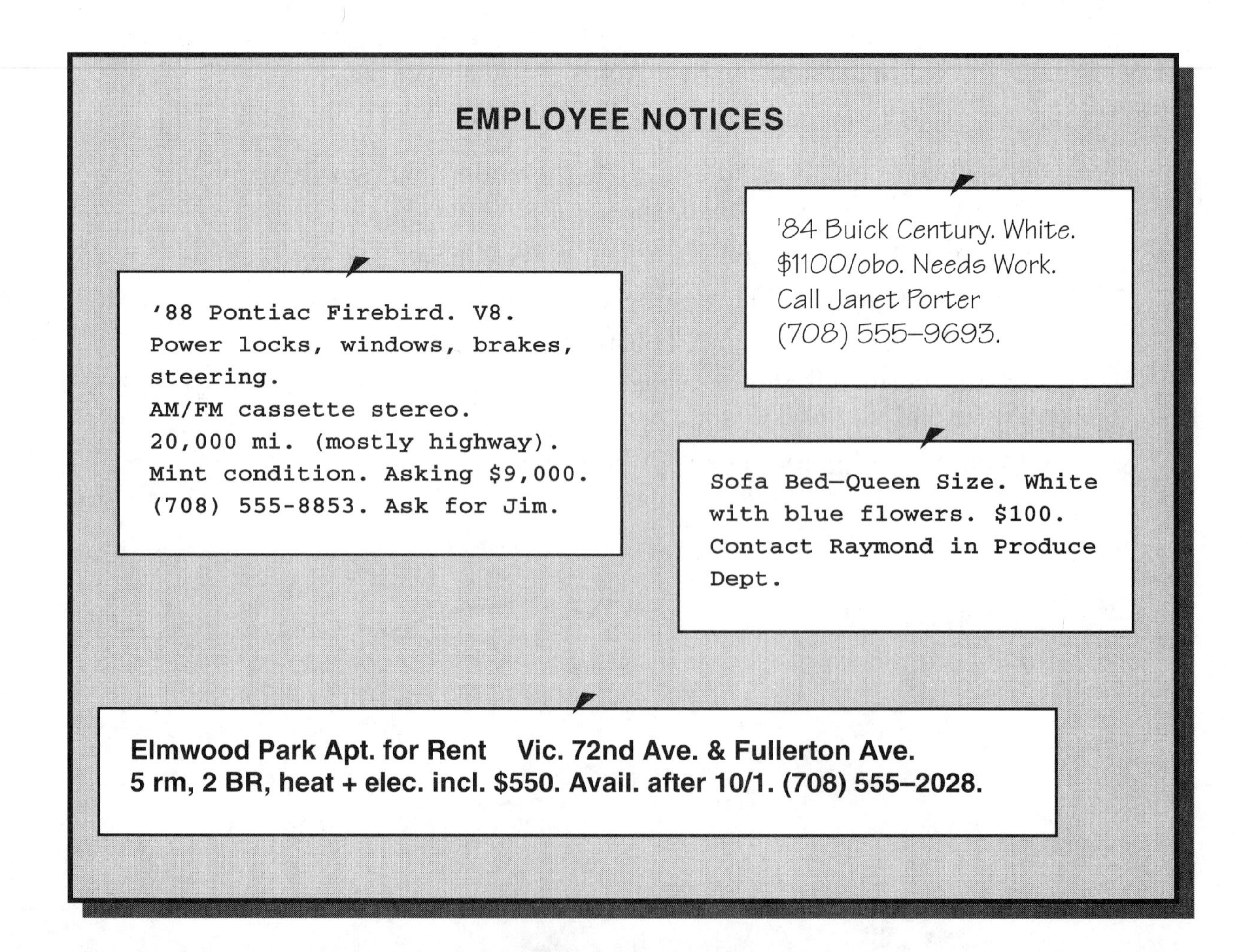

Understanding the Reading

(checking literal and inferential comprehension)

Answer the questions. Write on the lines.

1. Who is selling an '88 Pontiac Firebird? ____________________
2. Will Jim take less than $9,000 for his car? ____________________
3. Is the '84 Buick Century in mint condition? ____________________
4. What do you do if you want to look at the '84 Buick Century?

   ____
5. What size is Raymond's sofa bed? ____________________
6. How do you contact Raymond about the sofa bed? ____________________
7. Where is the Elmwood Park apartment that is for rent? ____________________
8. How many rooms and bedrooms are in the apartment? ____________________

Writing

(writing abbreviated messages in complete sentences, understanding abbreviations)

Choose two messages from the bulletin board. Write each message in sentences. Do not use abbreviations. Here is an example.

Janet Porter is selling her car. It is a 1984 Buick Century. It is white and it needs work. She wants $1100, but she will take the best offer. Call Janet at (708) 555-9693.

____

____

____

____

____

____

____

____

Listening

Activity #1 *(listening for specific information, writing prices)*

Lillian and Carmen, co-workers, are talking about a sale at Freddy's Finest Foods. Listen to the tape. Write the sale prices on the advertisement below.

Freddy's Finest Foods 10th Anniversary Special
10 Super Low Prices
Today Only!

Porterhouse Steak	____________	a pound
Freddy's Frozen Orange Juice	____________	for a 12-ounce can
Sweet Corn	____________	an ear
Red Potatoes	____________	a pound
Green or Red Grapes	____________	a pound
Wake-Up Coffee	____________	for a 26-ounce can
Thirsty Paper Towels	____________	a roll
Fresh-and-Tasty Turkey	____________	a pound
So-Soft Toilet Tissue	____________	for a 4-roll package
Country Fresh Cottage Cheese	____________	for a 24-ounce container

Activity #2 *(asking and answering questions about prices, listening for specific information)*

Ask your partner these questions. Listen to your partner and write the answers.

1. How much do you pay for a pound of tomatoes? ____________
2. How much do you pay for a pound of bananas? ____________
3. How much do you pay for a gallon of milk?____________
4. How much do you pay for a box of breakfast cereal? ____________
5. How much do you pay for a box of cookies? ____________

Using Math

(estimating numbers, adding decimals)

Sometimes you want to know "about" how much money you need. You can *estimate* or figure out "about" how much money by *rounding* numbers. If a number is between 1 and 4, you round the number down. If a number is between 5 and 9, you round the number up.

You can round prices to the nearest dollar. Look at the number in the tens place. Round up or down.

.98	round up to $ 1.00	$1.46	round down to $ 1.00
$5.59	round up to $ 6.00	$3.29	round down to $ 3.00
$10.72	round up to $11.00	$10.25	round down to $10.00

A. Round these prices to the nearest dollar.

1. green beans	1.59 _______	6. soap	.79 _______
2. broccoli	2.27 _______	7. shampoo	2.56 _______
3. lettuce	.69 _______	8. bread	1.12 _______
4. tomatoes	1.19 _______	9. ice cream	1.49 _______
5. candy	1.43 _______	10. pizza	3.89 _______

B. Here is the cash-register receipt for one of Lillian's customers. Add and write the subtotal. Add the subtotal and the tax and write the total. Now round the prices and tax to the nearest dollar. Write these estimates and add.

Freddy's Finest Foods

10/20/92 12:25 PM REG No. 11 OPR No. 29

Freddy's Froz OJ	.99
Sweet Corn 10 ears @ .12/ear	1.20
Wake-Up Coffee	3.79
So-Soft Toilet Tiss	1.19
CF Cottage Cheese	1.69
Choc chp cookies	1.79
Subtotal	_______
5% tax	.53
Total	_______

Estimate to the nearest dollar

Freddy's Froz OJ	_______
Sweet Corn 10 ears	_______
Wake-Up Coffee	_______
So-Soft Toilet Tiss	_______
CF Cottage Cheese	_______
Choc chp cookies	_______
Subtotal	_______
5% tax	_______
Total	_______

UNIT 5 *Interacting with Supervisors*

Before You Read

(making predictions, relating experiences to reading, establishing prior knowledge)

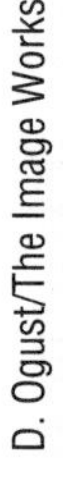

D. Ogust/The Image Works

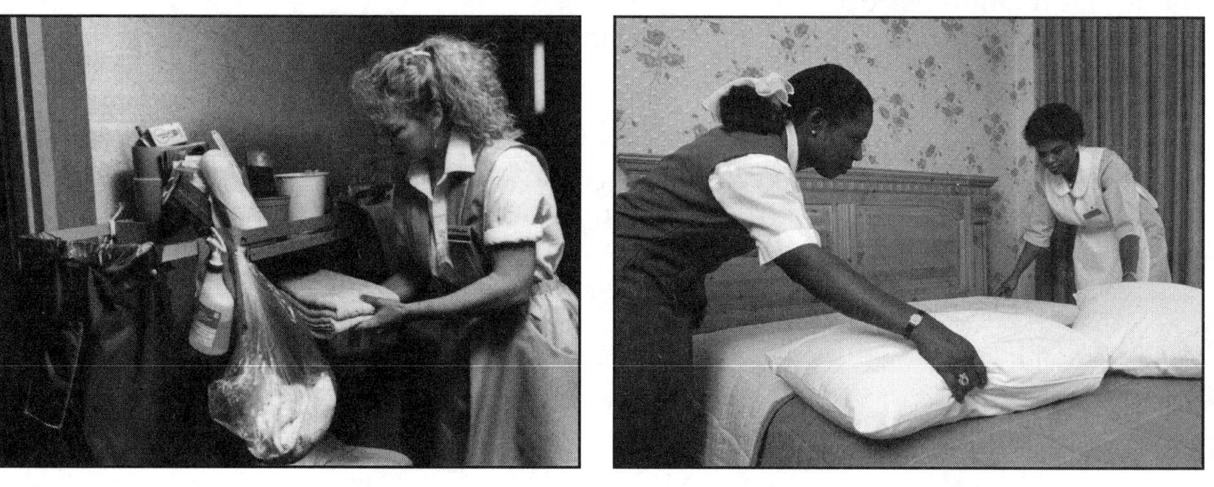

Richard Pasley/Stock Boston

Look at the pictures.

Talk about the pictures with a partner.

Read the questions.

Write the answers on the lines.

1. Where are the people in the pictures? ________________________________

2. What do you think is the job of the person in picture 1? ________________

   The people in picture 2? ____

3. What name do you use to call your friend at work? ____________________

4. What name do you use to call your supervisor at work? _________________

5. When do you use *Mr., Miss, Mrs.,* or *Ms.* with a person's last name? ______

   ____

Reading About Work

Welcome to the Sleepy Hollow Hotel

MRS. PALMER: Hello, Alberto. I'm Mrs. Palmer, the personnel manager.

ALBERTO: Hello, Mrs. Palmer.

MRS. PALMER: Welcome to the Sleepy Hollow Hotel. Here is your uniform. Wear a clean uniform every day you work.

ALBERTO: Thanks, Mrs. Palmer. I will.

MRS. PALMER: Okay, let's take a tour of the hotel. Here is the business office. Mr. Lopez, the day supervisor, works at this desk. He is somewhere in the hotel right now. At night, Ms. Schultz, the night supervisor, uses the same desk.This is Julie Barnes, the reservation clerk. She takes reservations from our customers and puts the information on the hotel computer. Julie, this is Alberto Hernandez.

JULIE: Hi, Alberto. Welcome.

ALBERTO: Hi, Ms. Barnes. Thank you.

JULIE: Oh, please call me Julie. Everyone does. Ms. Barnes sounds so formal.

ALBERTO: Okay, Julie. Thanks.

MRS. PALMER: See you later, Julie. We're going to see the rest of the hotel now. This is the front lobby. Today Jenna and Chris are working at the front desk. I'll introduce you later. They are busy with customers now. Over here is the housekeeping department, where you work. Today John, Young Lim, Rosa, Pedro, and George are working. Here is the gift shop and the pool. Next to the gift shop is the hotel manager's office.

Here's our hotel manager. Hi, Mr. Barrett. This is our new employee, Alberto Hernandez. Alberto, this is Mr. Barrett.

ALBERTO: Hello, Mr. Barrett. Thank you for giving me a job here.

MR. BARRETT: You're welcome, Alberto. I know you will do a good job for us. If you ever have a problem, talk to your supervisor first. If your supervisor can't help you, talk to Mrs. Palmer or me.

ALBERTO: Thanks, Mr. Barrett. I think I'll like working here.

Understanding New Words

(expanding vocabulary, using new words and phrases, identifying relationships between words)

A. Work with a partner. Read the words in the box. Find the words in the story on page 43. Circle the words.

personnel manager	uniform	supervisor	formal	lobby

B. Write a word from the box in the sentence.

1. Go to the ______________ ______________ if you want to apply for a job.
2. A person who looks after or directs workers is a ______________________.
3. A housekeeping employee wears a ________________. The work clothes all look the same.
4. I use an informal name when I talk to my friends. I use a ________________ name when I talk to my supervisors and people I don't know well.
5. A hotel _____________ has a front desk, and chairs and sofas to sit on.

C. Work with your partner. Cross out the word that does not belong.

1. worker ~~job~~ employee
2. supervisor boss receptionist
3. manager lobby entrance hall
4. uniform clothes paycheck
5. hotel personnel manager supervisor

"Perhaps you should speak to my supervisor."

Understanding the Reading

(checking literal and inferential comprehension)

A. Read the sentences with a partner. Decide together if they are true or false. Write *true* or *false* on the line.

1. Mrs. Palmer is Alberto's supervisor. ____________
2. Alberto works at the Happy Hollow Hotel. ____________
3. Alberto wears a uniform to work. ____________
4. Julie likes people to call her by her first name. ____________
5. Alberto calls Mrs. Palmer by her formal name. ____________
6. Jenna and Chris are busy at the front desk. ____________
7. The hotel manager's office is next to the lobby. ____________
8. Mr. Barrett is not in his office today. ____________
9. Mr. Barrett gives Alberto a tour of the hotel. ____________
10. Mr. Barrett tells Alberto to talk about a work problem with his supervisor first. ____________

B. There are five false sentences in Exercise A. Rewrite the false sentences to make them true.

1. Mrs. Palmer is the personnel manager.
2. ______________________________
3. ______________________________
4. ______________________________
5. ______________________________

Discussing

Activity #1 *(differentiating between formal and informal names, identifying and categorizing names)*

We use a person's informal name when the person is a friend, a part of our family, or the person asks us to use the informal name. The informal name is the first name or a nickname. *Robert* or *Bob* are informal names.

We use a person's formal name when we do business or when the person is not a close friend or a part of our family. The formal name is the title *Mr.* or *Mrs.* or *Ms.* with the person's last name. *Mrs. Palmer* and *Mr. Barrett* are formal names.

A. Work with your partner. Read the names and decide together if they are formal names or informal names. Write *formal name* or *informal name* on the lines.

1. Ms. Guzman ______________
2. Miguel ______________
3. Mr. Coleman ______________
4. Ms. Boyer ______________
5. Carmen ______________
6. Mrs. Chang ______________
7. Mrs. O'Henry ______________
8. Olivia ______________
9. Antonio ______________
10. Mr. Anderson ______________

The formal name for a married woman is *Mrs.* with the last name. If you do not know if the woman is married or single, use *Ms.* with the last name.

B. Circle the names of the married women in Exercise A. Underline the formal names of the other women.

C. Work with your partner. Write the formal names and the informal names of your co-workers and your supervisors. Do you use more informal names or formal names at your company? Talk about your answers with the class.

Informal names	**Formal Names**
______________	______________
______________	______________
______________	______________

Activity #2 *(introducing people, determining when to use a title in an introduction)*

Rules for Introducing People

1. Introduce the supervisor or manager to the employee. Say the name of the supervisor or manager first. Then say the name of the employee.
   Example: Mr. Barrett, this is Dolores. Dolores, this is our manager, Mr. Barrett.
2. Introduce an older person to a younger person. Say the name of the older person first. Then say the name of the younger person.
3. Introduce a woman to a man. Say the name of the woman first. Then say the name of the man.

Work with a small group of three students. Pretend you are the people below. One student introduces the other students to each other. Use the correct formal or informal name.

1. Introduce Maria (age 60) to Kathy (age 25).
2. Introduce Jeff (age 18) to Francisco (age 43).
3. Introduce Maureen Sanders (the day supervisor) to Lisa Martinez (new employee).
4. Introduce Harvey Thompson (president) to Karen Bell (secretary, married).
5. Introduce Karen Bell (secretary, married) to George Davis (reservation clerk).
6. Introduce Nora O'Leary (manager, single) to Jose Garcia (accountant).

Activity #3 *(using creative thinking skills in a role play, empathizing with a character)*

1. Partner A is the employee. Partner B is the supervisor. The employee thinks that his or her paycheck is not correct. The employee did not get paid for a holiday and for two hours of overtime. The employee goes to the supervisor to ask about the mistake.
2. Partner B is the new employee. Partner A is the supervisor. They are eating lunch together and talking about the hotel where they work. The supervisor invites the employee to call him or her by his or her first name.

Reading at Work

Understanding New Words

(expanding vocabulary, understanding and using words in context)

Read the sentences below. Find and circle the underlined words in the following reading.

1. In a memo, Re: means "regarding." This tells what the memo is about.
2. Employees are required to work one weekend per month. Each month, it is necessary for every employee to work one weekend.
3. Clothes that are wrinkled need to be pressed with an iron to make them smooth.
4. The hotel issues, or gives, each employee one uniform.
5. Taxes are deducted from each paycheck. The tax money is taken out of the check.
6. Contact your supervisor when you have a problem. Talk to your supervisor in person or on the telephone.

Many companies use memos to communicate to their employees. Read the memo below.

Sleepy Hollow Hotel

901 Sandman Street Chicago, IL 60621 (312) 555–1000

To: All Housekeeping Employees
From: Guy Lopez, Day Supervisor
Date: April 12, 1993
Re: Uniforms

Uniforms are required for all housekeeping employees during working hours. Uniforms should be clean and pressed if needed.

The Sleepy Hollow Hotel issues one uniform per employee.

You may purchase additional shirts, pants or dresses. Cost per shirt is $10.50. Pants are $15.00. Dresses are $22.00. Payment will be deducted from your paycheck.

To order additional uniforms, contact Mrs. Palmer in the Personnel Office.

Understanding the Reading

(checking literal comprehension)

Answer the questions. Write on the lines.

1. Who is the memo for?____________________
2. Who is the memo from? ____________________
3. Do the employees pay for their first uniform? ____________________
4. How much do employees pay for additional uniform shirts?____________

   additional uniform pants? __________ additional uniform dresses? __________
5. How does an employee pay for additional uniforms?

   ____
6. What do employees do if they want additional uniforms? ____________

Writing

(reading and completing a memo)

Complete the memo below with your additional uniform order.

To: Mrs. Palmer, Personnel Manager

From: ____________________

Date: ____________________

Re: Additional Uniforms

Please order the following additional uniforms for me.

Quantity	*Item*	*Size*	*Price per Item*	*Total*
	pants		15.00	
	shirts		10.50	
	dresses		22.00	
Total deducted from next paycheck ____________________				

Listening

Activity #1 *(listening to verify specific information)*

A customer calls two hotels to find out about hotel services and prices. Listen to the tape. Put a check (✔) for each service that the hotel has.

	Sleepy Hollow Hotel	*Budget Quality Motel*
TV		
cable TV channels		
AM/FM radio		
air-conditioning		
parking		
swimming pool		
video games		
exercise room		
conference rooms		
coffee shop		
restaurant		
vending machines		
babysitter		

Activity #2 *(listening for prices)*

Listen to the tape again. Write the prices on the lines.

	Sleepy Hollow Hotel	*Budget Quality Motel*
1. Single room		
2. Double room		
3. Cable TV channels		
4. Babysitter for one child		
5. Babysitter for two children		

Using Math

(problem solving, determining when to use addition, subtraction, multiplication, or division)

Read the problems. Circle *add, subtract, multiply,* or *divide.* You can circle more than one word. Solve the problems.

	To solve the problem, I need to:
1. Alberto makes $7.00 an hour. He works 40 hours a week. How much money does Alberto make in one week? ____________	*add* *subtract* *multiply* *divide*
2. If Alberto works over 40 hours, he gets overtime. Overtime pay is time and a half. This means Alberto gets the regular pay of $7.00 an hour + one-half of $7.00 an hour. How much money does Alberto make for overtime? __________ per hour	*add* *subtract* *multiply* *divide*
3. Alberto worked 5 hours of overtime this week. How much money did he make only for the overtime hours? ____________	*add* *subtract* *multiply* *divide*
4. Alberto worked 42 hours, 40 hours, 40 hours, and 43 hours for this month. How many hours did Alberto work this month? __________	*add* *subtract* *multiply* *divide*
5. Alberto makes $560.00 every two weeks. He pays $140.00 in federal taxes, $39.20 in state taxes. How much does he get in his paycheck after the taxes are deducted? __________	*add* *subtract* *multiply* *divide*
6. Alberto pays $45.00 for medical insurance and orders 2 uniform shirts and 1 pair of uniform pants. The shirts cost $10.50 each and the pants are $15.00. How much money will be deducted from his check for insurance and uniforms?______	*add* *subtract* *multiply* *divide*

UNIT 6 *Personalities and Conflicts*

Before You Read
(making predictions, relating experiences to reading, establishing prior knowledge)

Look at the pictures.

Talk about the pictures with a partner.

Read the questions.

Write the answers on the lines.

1. Where are the employees in the cartoons? ______________________
2. What do you think the employees are doing wrong? ______________________
3. Which employee do you want to be your partner on the job? ______________________

   Why? ______________________
4. When you do something wrong at work, what do other employees say to you? ______________________

Reading About Work

Production Problems at Epic Electronics

"This morning we have some bad news," said Mr. Sullivan, the vice-president of production. "Epic Electronics is losing money. Our production is down from last year. Our profits are down. About the only thing that is not down is our percentage of defects. We need to increase production and decrease defects. I want each division to think of some ideas to help us meet these goals. Put your heads together and let me know what you come up with."

"Did you hear that guy?" Buddy said to his partner on the production line. "He wants us to do all the work and come up with all the ideas, too. What's he getting paid for anyway? I get paid for the work I do. If Epic Electronics wants more work from me, they will have to pay me more money. And it wouldn't hurt to replace some of this old, broken-down equipment. How can we work when our machines keep breaking?"

In another part of the company, Vary and his partner are also discussing the company's problems. "I didn't know about the production problems," Vary said. "Maybe we can help. If we work in teams of two or four, we can work faster. Every two hours we can change places on the production line. Then we won't get so tired, and maybe we won't make so many mistakes. I don't want to lose my job here. I don't want my friends here to lose their jobs, either."

Understanding New Words and Phrases

(expanding vocabulary, understanding and using new words and idioms)

A. Work with a partner. Read the words in the box. Find and circle the words in the story on page 53.

come up with	put your heads together	decrease	increase
defects	vice-president	losing	profit

B. Write a word from the box in the sentence.

1. The ________________ reports to the president.
2. To ________________ production means to make more products.
3. To ________________ production means to make fewer products.
4. The money a company makes after paying their costs is the ____________.
5. The opposite of making money is ____________ money.
6. Think of a new idea. See what you can ________ ____ ________.
7. Mistakes or problems with a product are called ________________.
8. Work with a small group to think of the answers. Try to ________ ________ ________ ________ so you have many people working to think of the answers.

C. Write the words from Exercise B in the puzzle. Write one letter on each line.

6. c o m e u p w i t h
8. _ _ _ _ _ _ _ _ _ _ _ _ _ _ _ _ _ _ _ _
2. _ _ _ _ _ _ _ _
4. _ _ _ _ _ _ _
5. _ _ _ _ _ _
1. _ _ _ - _ _ _ _ _ _ _ _ _
3. _ _ _ _ _ _ _ _
7. _ _ _ _ _ _ _

D. The letters in the boxes in Exercise C make a word. Write the word in the sentence.

Employees sometimes have a ________________ with other employees or supervisors at work.

Understanding the Reading

(checking literal and inferential comprehension, analyzing motives for actions)

Read the questions. Write the answers on the lines.

1. Who is the vice-president of Epic Electronics? ____________________

2. What two things are down this year at Epic Electronics? ____________________

   ____

3. What one thing is up at Epic Electronics? ____________________

4. Why does Mr. Sullivan want each division to put their heads together?

   ____

5. Does Buddy like Mr. Sullivan's suggestion? ________ Why or why not?

   ____

6. What are Buddy's two suggestions to increase production? ____________

   ____

7. Why does Vary suggest working in teams of two or four? ____________

   ____

8. Why does Vary suggest changing places on the production line? ________

   ____

9. Do you like Buddy's suggestions or Vary's suggestions? __________ Why?

   ____

10. Do you think Mr. Sullivan will like Buddy's suggestions or Vary's suggestions? ________________ Why? ____________________

Discussing

Activity #1 *(differentiating between statements that accept criticism or reject criticism)*

Sometimes a supervisor or co-worker tells you about something you are doing wrong. This is *criticism* of your work. Some workers accept criticism or suggestions. Other workers reject (do not accept) criticism or suggestions very well.

Work with a partner. Read the sentences and questions. Circle *accepts criticism* or *rejects criticism.*

1.	Can you show me how to do this again?	*accepts criticism*	*rejects criticism*
2.	I'm sorry.	*accepts criticism*	*rejects criticism*
3.	Mind your own business.	*accepts criticism*	*rejects criticism*
4.	There's nothing wrong with my work.	*accepts criticism*	*rejects criticism*
5.	I work slowly at first. I'll try to work faster now.	*accepts criticism*	*rejects criticism*
6.	Is this the right way to run the machine?	*accepts criticism*	*rejects criticism*
7.	I don't like the way you're talking to me.	*accepts criticism*	*rejects criticism*
8.	If you don't like the way I do it, do it yourself.	*accepts criticism*	*rejects criticism*
9.	Let me see if I understand what you want me to do.	*accepts criticism*	*rejects criticism*
10.	Now I understand. I'll do it right this time.	*accepts criticism*	*rejects criticism*

Activity #2 *(using creative thinking skills in role plays, empathizing with a character)*

Work with your partner. Show and tell what happens.

1. Partners A and B are co-workers and partners at a factory. Partner A is very tired and keeps forgetting to check the products for defects. Partner B is a new employee and wants to do a good job. Partner B thinks he or she might lose this job if there are too many defects in the products. Partner B gives suggestions to Partner A. Partner A accepts the suggestions.
2. Partner B is the supervisor. Partner A is an employee who makes many mistakes. The supervisor criticizes the employee. The employee rejects the criticism.
3. Partner A is the supervisor. Partner B is an employee who makes two mistakes in one day. The supervisor criticizes the employee. The employee accepts the criticism.

Reading at Work

Understanding New Words

(expanding vocabulary, understanding and using new words and phrases)

Read the sentences below. Find and circle the underlined words in the following reading.

1. You compliment me when you tell me that I do excellent work.
2. State your name and address. "My name is Julia Fisher. My address is 11204 South Maplewood Avenue in Oak Lawn."
3. Josef is talking. Before Josef finishes talking, Gilberto interrupts him to ask about a problem with a machine.
4. "Break time is now over. I repeat, break time is now over."
5. Our machines are not working. Another equipment failure like this will hurt our production.

All companies want to solve problems and correct mistakes. Here is a list of things to do to solve problems.

10 Steps to Solve Problems

1. Before you criticize, compliment the other worker on something he or she does well.
2. Offer criticism of the action, not of the person.
3. State the problem clearly.
4. Ask, "What can I do to help you solve this problem?"
5. Listen without interrupting.
6. If you don't understand, ask questions.
7. Repeat a new instruction to make sure you understand it.
8. Ask for help when you need it.
9. Report machine or equipment failures to supervisors immediately.
10. Compliment the other worker when the problem is corrected.

Understanding the Reading

(applying reading to a new context, using critical-thinking skills to solve problems)

Read the sentences and questions. Write the number or numbers of the problem-solving steps.

Problem-Solving Steps

1. "Henry, you work well with Luis. Now let's talk about how you can work well with Ed." ____________
2. "What can I do to help you solve this problem?" ____________
3. "I don't understand what you said. Can you explain it to me again, please?" ____________
4. "Eva, the problem is that you don't clean your work area before you go home." ____________
5. "Put each product in a separate bag. Write the date. Then write your name on the checklist." "OK, I put the product in a bag, write the date, and then write my name on the checklist." ____________
6. "Mrs. Williams, can you help me? I have a problem with my machine." ____________
7. "Henry, I see that you and Ed are working well together. You corrected that problem right away." ____________

Writing

(identifying and writing a problem, identifying a possible solution to a problem)

1. Write one problem you have with another person at work. ____________

   ____

   ____

2. How can you correct this problem? ____________________

   ____

Listening

(listening for specific information, determining appropriate responses in work situations)

Listen to the tape. Circle the sentence that you think is best.

1. Oh, what's the problem, Mr. Morton?
   Fix it yourself. I'm busy now.
2. I'll be there in about an hour.
   Sure, Mrs. Perry. I'll be right there.
3. No, Mr. Lennon, I don't. Will you explain it again to me?
   No, but it can't be too difficult. Let me try it.
4. All the other secretaries take more than 15 minutes.
   I'm sorry, Ms. Brennan. I will be back in 15 minutes from now on.
5. I guess I will come to work on Friday, then. I want to get paid for the holiday.
   Who cares about the company's policies! I want a long weekend.
6. Don't tell me that I put it in the wrong place. Maybe you are looking for it in the wrong place.
   I put it in the supply room on the second floor. I'll go and get it for you.
7. I'll put out my cigarette. I didn't know there was no smoking in this area. Next time, I'll go to the cafeteria.
   You nonsmokers are always making trouble. Leave us smokers alone.
8. I can't do everything. Get someone else to check the boxes.
   I'll check every box, Rosemary. I'm sorry about that.

Using Math and a Line Graph

(interpreting a line graph, calculating percents, changing decimals to percents)

This is a line graph. Read the title. Look at the numbers on the left side of the graph. These are the number of televisions at Epic Electronics. Read the words at the bottom of the graph. These are the months of the year. Find the line that shows the production (the televisions made). Find the line that shows the defects (the number of televisions with mistakes or problems).

Epic Electronics Yearly Report of Production and Defects: Model TV 2000

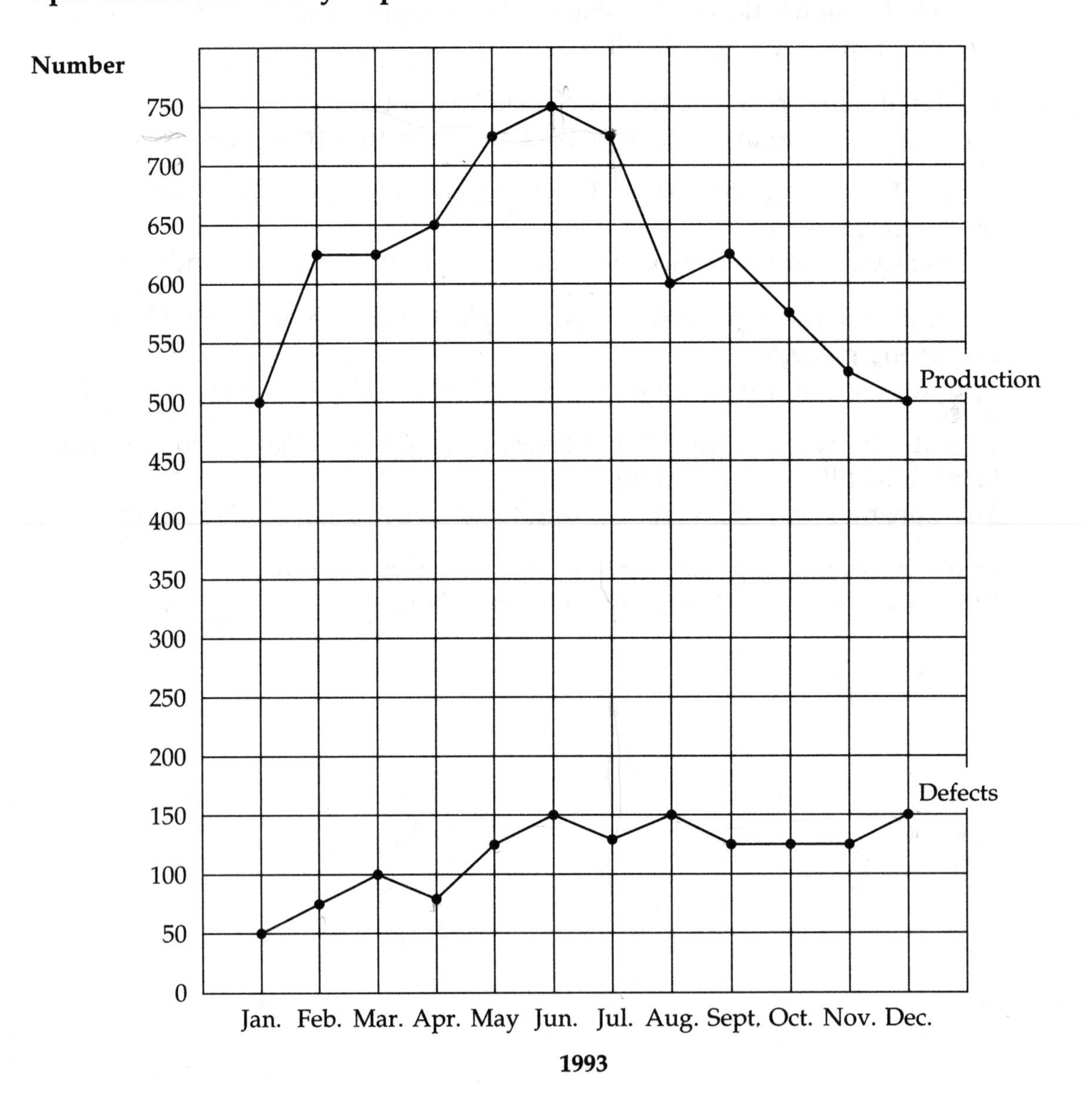

Answer the questions.

1. How many televisions were produced in January? ______________
2. How many televisions were produced in July? ______________
3. What month had the most production? ______________
4. What months had the least production? ______________
5. How many defects were there in the televisions produced in March? ______________
6. How many defects were there in the televisions produced in December? ______________
7. What months had the most defects? ______________
8. What month had the least defects? ______________

Figure the percentage of defects for June. Divide the number of defects in June by the number of televisions produced in June.

Example: 150 defects ÷ 750 televisions = .20

Change the decimal to a percent. Move the decimal point two places to the right.

Example: .20 = 20% .50 = 50% .37 = 37%

9. What is the percentage of defects for August? ______________
10. What is the percentage of defects for December? ______________

UNIT 7 *Valued Work Behaviors/Qualities*

Before You Read

(making predictions, relating experiences to reading, establishing prior knowledge)

A.T.&T. Co. Photo Center

Look at the picture.

Talk about the picture with a partner.

Read the questions.

Write the answers on the lines.

1. What is the employee in the picture receiving? ______________________
2. Why is he receiving the award? ______________________

   ____
3. What does your company do to reward excellent employees? ____________

   ____

Reading About Work

Susan's Special Night

"Susan is very nervous tonight," Carol whispers to her friend Howard.

"She is a candidate for Employee of the Year," Howard says. "Her supervisor thinks she is very responsible. She does the most work in her department, and she always finishes on time. She doesn't make many mistakes."

"Does Susan miss many days of work?" Carol asks.

"No, she has a perfect attendance record this year. That is one of the things the president looks at when he decides who will be Employee of the Year," Howard says. "Wait, here's the president. I think he's going to make the announcement!"

"Good evening, ladies and gentlemen," the company president begins. "Every year we present the Employee of the Year award at our annual company Christmas party. As you know, the winner receives a free weekend and meals at the Fantasy Inn. This year our profits are up, so I am also giving the winner a bonus check for $200.00.

"It is a pleasure to present the award for Employee of the Year to one of our most dependable and responsible employees. This employee comes to work every day. She works well with the other employees in her department. She is happy and smiling every time I see her. She does her work quickly, completely, and corrrectly. Please welcome Peppermill Papers' Employee of the Year—Susan Spencer!"

Understanding New Words

(expanding vocabulary, understanding and using new words)

A. Work with a partner. Read the words in the box. Find the words in the story on page 63. Circle the words.

candidate	announcement	award	annual	responsible

B. Read the sentences. Circle *a* or *b*.

1. A candidate for Employee of the Year is
   a. a person who wants to win the Employee of the Year award.
   b. a person who decides who is Employee of the Year.
2. Marta makes an announcement that she is having a baby in October. Marta
   a. tells all the people that she is having a baby in October.
   b. writes a memo about women having babies.
3. Susan receives an award as Employee of the Year. An award is
   a. a day off from work.
   b. a prize or special reward for doing excellent work.
4. Every year, Peppermill Papers has an annual company Christmas party.
   a. The party is only one time every year.
   b. The party is every day of the year.
5. A responsible employee comes to work every day on time. "Responsible" means
   a. to do all the work and follow all the rules.
   b. to call a friend when you are late.

Understanding the Reading

(evaluating information to make a judgment, checking literal and inferential comprehension)

Read these sentences with a partner. Decide together if they are **true** or **false** or if there is **not enough information** to answer. Put a check (✔) in the column.

		True	False	Not Enough Information
1.	Susan works in the office.		✓	
2.	Susan is a candidate for Employee of the Year.	✓		
3.	Susan is absent one day every month.		✓	
4.	Susan enjoys the food at the Fantasy Inn.			✓
5.	The president is giving extra money to the Employee of the Year.	✓		
6.	Carol and Howard work in the same department.			✓
7.	Peppermill Papers has an annual picnic.		✓	

Discussing

Activity #1 *(completing a conversation, using critical thinking)*

The president of Peppermill Papers gives the award for Employee of the Year to Susan Spencer. With a partner, decide what Susan says to the president. Write Susan's words on the lines.

PRESIDENT: Congratulations, Susan. You receive a free weekend at the Fantasy Inn.

SUSAN: ____

PRESIDENT: And here is your bonus check for $200.00. What will you do with the bonus?

SUSAN: ____

PRESIDENT: That's a great idea. What will you tell other employees who want to be Employee of the Year?

SUSAN: ____

PRESIDENT: Thank you, Susan. Enjoy your award. You are a hard-working and responsible employee. We are lucky to have you at Peppermill Papers.

Activity #2 *(describing characteristics, presenting and supporting an opinion, making judgments, establishing criteria for evaluation)*

Discuss these questions with a partner.

1. What makes a person an excellent employee?
2. How can you be a responsible employee at your company?
3. Who do you think is a good candidate for Employee of the Year at your company? Why?
4. You are president of your company. What award do you give to the Employee of the Year? How do you choose the Employee of the Year?

Reading at Work

Understanding New Words

(expanding vocabulary, understanding and using new words)

Read the sentences below. Find and circle the underlined words in the following reading.

1. The new hotel is very luxurious. It has fancy carpet on the floor. There are beautiful lights. There are fresh flowers and chocolates in every room.
2. Elsa describes her new uniform. "My uniform is a green dress with white stripes."
3. Elvin trains new employees. He shows them what work to do. He tells them where to get supplies. He shows them how to work the machines.
4. I look for ways to improve my company. I want to make my company better.
5. Genda deserves a vacation next month. She is working every day this month.

Some companies have a newsletter with articles about the company and the employees. Read this article about the Employee of the Year.

SUSAN SPENCER NAMED EMPLOYEE OF THE YEAR

Susan Spencer is Peppermill Papers' Employee of the Year for 1993. As the winner of this award, Susan receives a weekend at the luxurious new Fantasy Inn. In addition, Susan receives a bonus check for $200.00. What will Susan do with the extra money?

"I want to study computers. There is a class at Triton College beginning in January. I think I will take the class. The bonus money will pay for the class and the books," Susan said after receiving her award at the company Christmas party on December 20, 1993.

Susan's supervisor describes her as "hard-working and dependable."

"If there is an important job to do, I give it to Susan," her supervisor, Ms. Montoya says. "I know she will do a good job. Susan has an excellent attendance record. She trains new employees. She looks for ways to improve the company. I'm glad she is the winner of the award. She deserves it."

Congratulations, Susan!

Understanding the Reading

(checking literal comprehension)

Answer the questions. Write on the lines.

1. What does Susan want to study? ______________________
2. What will Susan do with the bonus money? ______________________
3. How does Susan's supervisor describe her? ______________________

Writing

(completing a recommendation form, substantiating opinions)

Complete the recommendation form for Employee of the Year. Write about an employee from your company. Use your name as the supervisor.

Recommendation Form for Employee of the Year

I recommend ______________________ as Employee of the Year for the year______.

I think this person is an excellent employee because______________________

____

____

____

Number of days absent this year __________ Number of times late to work _______

Supervisor's signature ______________________

Listening

(using aural discrimination skills, listening for specific information, using context clues to aid listening comprehension)

Listen to the tape of the company president. Circle the words you hear.

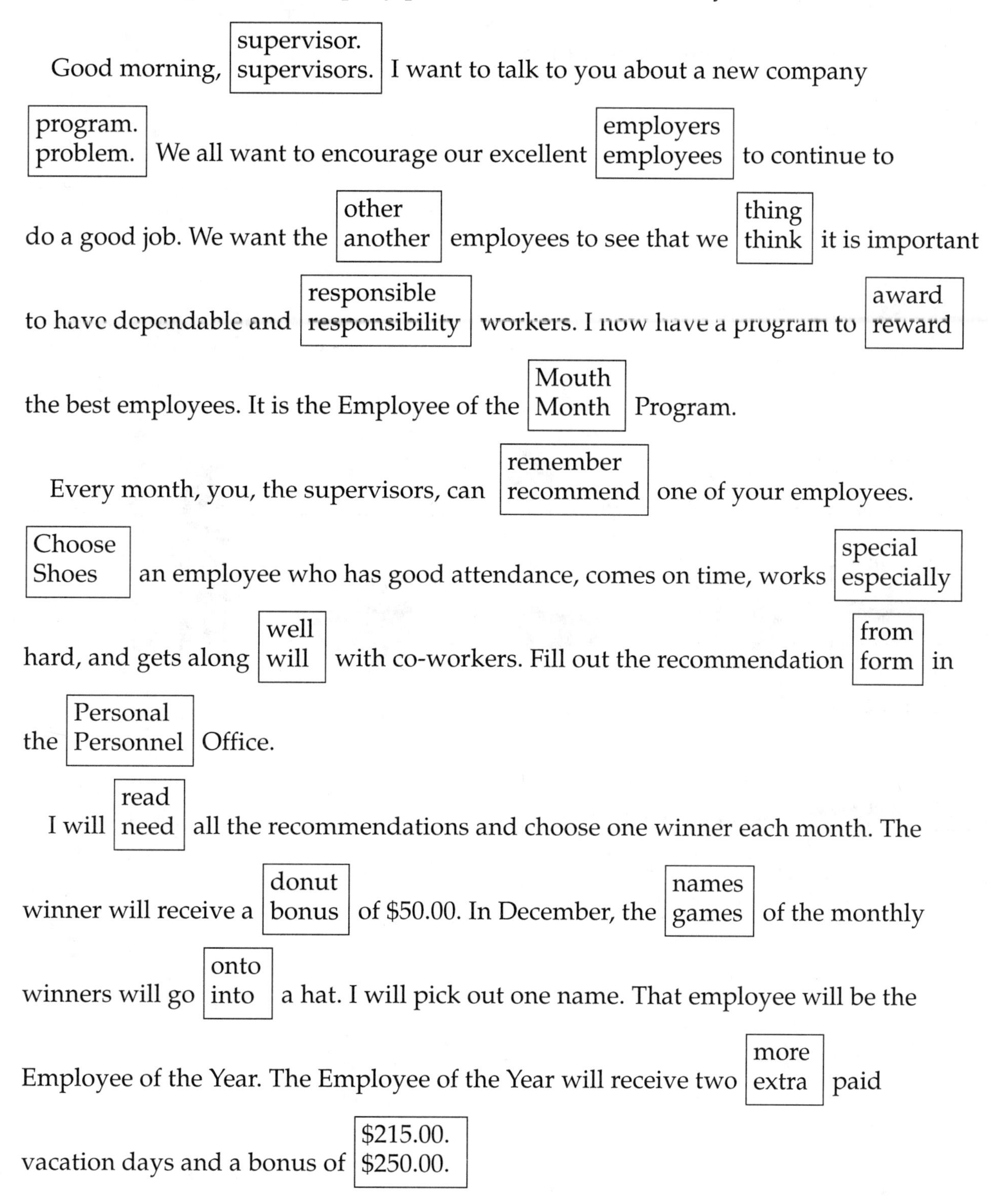

Good morning, [supervisor. / supervisors.] I want to talk to you about a new company [program. / problem.] We all want to encourage our excellent [employers / employees] to continue to do a good job. We want the [other / another] employees to see that we [thing / think] it is important to have dependable and [responsible / responsibility] workers. I now have a program to [award / reward] the best employees. It is the Employee of the [Mouth / Month] Program.

Every month, you, the supervisors, can [remember / recommend] one of your employees. [Choose / Shoes] an employee who has good attendance, comes on time, works [special / especially] hard, and gets along [well / will] with co-workers. Fill out the recommendation [from / form] in the [Personal / Personnel] Office.

I will [read / need] all the recommendations and choose one winner each month. The winner will receive a [donut / bonus] of $50.00. In December, the [names / games] of the monthly winners will go [onto / into] a hat. I will pick out one name. That employee will be the Employee of the Year. The Employee of the Year will receive two [more / extra] paid vacation days and a bonus of [$215.00. / $250.00.]

Using Math and a Bar Graph

(reading and interpreting a bar graph, adding and multiplying to solve problems)

Read the title of t[illegible]llars on the left side of the graph. Read the c[illegible]h. Read the key.

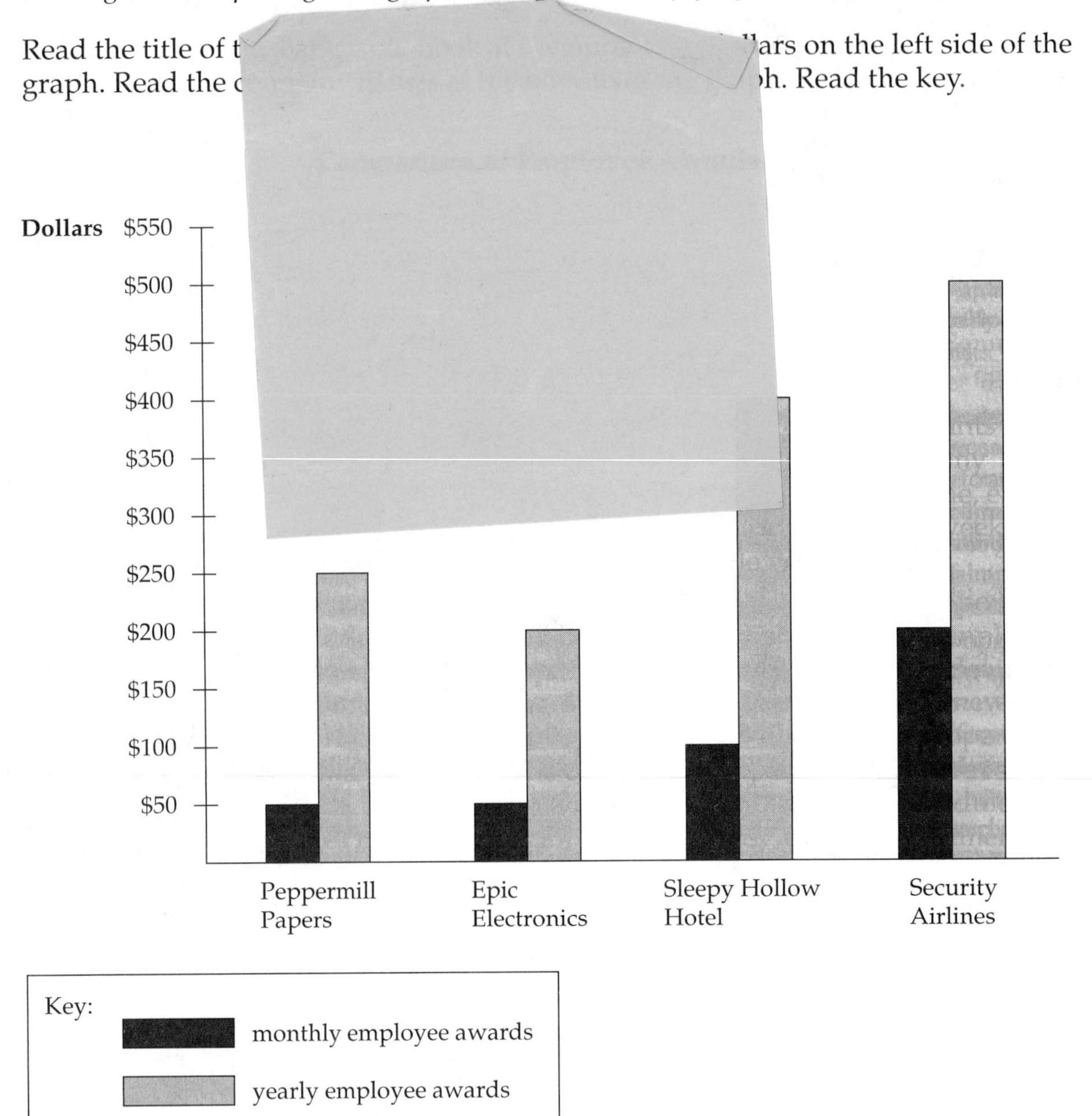

Answer the questions.

1. How much does Peppermill Papers spend on monthly employee awards? ____________ On yearly employee awards? ____________
2. How much does Sleepy Hollow Hotel spend on monthly employee awards? ____________ On yearly employee awards? ____________
3. How much does Epic Electronics spend on monthly employee awards for one year? (*Hint:* Multiply monthly employee award $50 X 12 months = ?) ____________
4. How much does Security Airlines spend on 12 monthly employee awards and one yearly employee award? ____________
5. How much does Peppermill Papers spend in one year on all its employee awards? ____________
6. How much does Sleepy Hollow Hotel spend in one year on all its employee awards? ____________

UNIT 8 *Job Performance*

Before You Read

(making predictions, relating experiences to reading, establishing prior knowledge)

Look at the pictures.

Talk about the pictures with a partner.

Read the questions.

Write the answers on the lines.

1. What do you see in picture 1? ____________________

   In picture 2? ____________________
2. How do you think the employee in picture 1 feels? ____________________

   How do you think the employee in picture 2 feels? ____________________
3. When does your supervisor evaluate you (tell you if you are doing a good job or a bad job)? ____________________

Reading About Work

Eva's Evaluation

Mrs. Nelson, the manager of Thrifty Department Store calls Eva into her office.

MRS. NELSON: Hi, Eva. It's time for your six-month evaluation.

EVA: What's a six-month evaluation?

MRS. NELSON: An evaluation is when I tell you about the things you do well in your job. I also tell about the things you need to improve. All our employees have an annual evaluation. New employees also have a six-month evaluation."

EVA: Oh, now I understand.

MRS. NELSON: Eva, I like the way you help the customers. You smile and listen to them. You try to answer their questions.You also do a good job putting the stock on the shelves and putting the price signs where the customers can read them.

EVA: Thanks, Mrs. Nelson.

MRS. NELSON: There are two things I want you to improve. When you hear a cashier call for a price check, go immediately to help. Our customers don't like to wait at the cashier. Also, when there is a problem with the stock, come to me immediately. Don't wait. If I'm not here, write a note and put it on my desk.

Keep up the good work. Your next check will have a 50¢ per hour raise. Now please sign your evaluation form.

EVA: Okay and thanks, Mrs. Nelson.

Understanding New Words

(expanding vocabulary, understanding and using new words and phrases)

A. Work with a partner. Read the words in the box. Find the words in the story on page 73. Circle the words.

evaluation	stock	price check	immediately	raise

B. Work with your partner. Cross out the word or phrase that does not belong.

1. things a store sells stock responsible
2. right now later immediately
3. annual increase in money raise

C. Match the words with their meanings. Draw a line.

Words	Meanings
1. evaluation	without waiting; right now
2. price check	the things a store sells
3. immediately	to ask for the price of something that has no price on it
4. stock	a supervisor's opinion about how well or poorly you do a job
5. raise	an increase in the money you make

Understanding the Reading

(checking literal and inferential comprehension, identifying a character's feelings)

Fill in the circle that answers the question.

1. Who is Eva's manager?

   ● Mrs. Nelson
   ❍ Mr. Nelson
   ❍ Miss Nelson

2. What is the name of the store where Eva works?

   ❍ Thirsty Department Store
   ❍ Thrifty Department Store
   ❍ Thirty Department Store

3. When do new employees have an evaluation?

   ❍ after six years
   ❍ after six weeks
   ❍ after six months

4. Why do employees have evaluations?

   ❍ to find out what they do well and what they need to improve
   ❍ because Mrs. Nelson likes to talk to the employees
   ❍ to decide who is Employee of the Year

5. Why do employees sign their evaluation forms?

   ❍ to show the employee likes the evaluation
   ❍ to show the employee knows how to write
   ❍ to show the employee understands the evaluation

6. How do you think Eva feels about her evaluation?

   ❍ happy to receive a good evaluation and a raise
   ❍ tired because she works very hard
   ❍ angry because Mrs. Nelson tells her things to improve

Discussing

Activity #1 *(completing a conversation, understanding and using context clues)*

Hiroshi goes to see his supervisor about his evaluation. With a partner, decide what Hiroshi and Mr. Murray say. Write the words on the lines.

MR. MURRAY: Hi, Hiroshi. What can I do for you?

HIROSHI: I'm here for my ____________ evaluation. Your secretary says ____.

MR. MURRAY: Well, now is not a good time for me. I have a meeting with ____________________ in five minutes. Can you come back ____________________?

HIROSHI: Sure. Tomorrow is fine. What time is good for you?

MR. MURRAY: How about ___________? That is before I have to go to see _____________. I will need ________ minutes to talk to you.

HIROSHI: Okay, Mr. Murray. I'll see you __________________ at ____________.

Activity #2 *(using creative thinking skills in role plays, empathizing with a character)*

Work with a partner. Act out what happens.

1. Student A is the supervisor. Student B is the employee. The supervisor evaluates the employee. The supervisor tells 2 good things the employee does. The supervisor also tells 2 things the employee can do to improve.
2. Student A is the supervisor. Student B is the company president. The company president evaluates the supervisor. The company president tells many things the supervisor can do to improve. The supervisor doesn't like to hear these things.

Activity #3 *(relating reading to actual experience, identifying personal strengths and weaknesses)*

Discuss these questions with a partner.

1. When do employees at your company receive evaluations?
2. When do employees at your company receive raises?
3. Who evaluates you?
4. What are the things you do well in your job (your strengths)?
5. What are the things you need to improve in your job (your weaknesses)?

Reading at Work

Understanding New Words

(expanding vocabulary, understanding and using new words)

Read the sentences below. Find and circle the underlined words in the following reading.

1. Punctual means to be on time. Supervisors like a punctual employee.
2. An accurate employee does not make mistakes.
3. Your appearance is the way your hair, skin, and clothes look. Parents want their children to have a good appearance.
4. We communicate by talking, reading, and writing.
5. Susan is an efficient office worker. She works quickly on the computer. She finishes all her work in a short time.

Many companies use an evaluation form. Read the evaluation form below.

Employee Evaluation Form

Employee's Name________________________ Date____________

Department ______________ Job Title ______________________

	Always	*Usually*	*Sometimes*	*Rarely*	*Never*
1. Is the employee punctual? Does the employee arrive on time for work?	5	4	3	2	1
2. Is the employee's appearance neat and clean?	5	4	3	2	1
3. Is the employee responsible and dependable?	5	4	3	2	1
4. Is the employee accurate? Does the employee work without making many mistakes?	5	4	3	2	1
5. Is the employee efficient? Does the employee finish the work in the required time?	5	4	3	2	1
6. Does the employee communicate problems immediately to a supervisor?	5	4	3	2	1
7. Is the employee friendly and pleasant to customers and other employees?	5	4	3	2	1

Supervisor's Signature ____________________

Employee's Signature ____________________

Understanding the Reading

(checking literal and inferential comprehension, making judgments, substantiating an opinion)

Answer the questions. Write on the lines.

1. What number means *always* on the evaluation? ____________
2. What number means *never* on the evaluation? ____________
3. What does *rarely* mean? ____________
4. In the evaluation, what question do you think is most important? ____________

   Why? ____________

Writing

(completing sentences with new vocabulary words, writing about personal strengths and weaknesses, using present-tense verbs)

Complete these sentences.

1. A punctual employee comes to work on time.
2. An efficient employee ____________.
3. An accurate employee ____________.
4. A friendly employee ____________.
5. In my job, my strengths are that I ____________

   ____________.
6. In my job, my weaknesses are that I ____________

   ____________.

Listening

Activity #1 *(listening for names and numbers)*

Listen to the tape. Cashiers are calling for price checks on different things. Write the register number. Circle the items that need price checks. Write the prices.

1. Register Number ______ Hollywood Videotapes $__________
   Hollywood Cassette Tapes
   Halloween plates

2. Register Number ______ Quickly Clean Room $__________
   Quick 'n Clean Broom
   Chicken Balloon

3. Register Number ______ Emergency Pain Pills $__________
   Allergy Tablets
   Energy Plus Daily Vitamins

4. Register Number ______ Phone-A-Friend Car Telephone $__________
   Phone Friend Answering Machine
   Phone Friend Telephone

5. Register Number ______ trash can $ __________
   trash bags
   cash box

Activity #2 *(listening for numbers and letters, using auditory discrimination skills)*

Listen to the tape. Eva and Hiroshi are checking the numbers of stock items. Circle the numbers you hear.

1.	A 16 002	E 60 002	5.	B 15 012	V 50 012
2.	I 17 013	E 70 013	6.	M 90 064	N 19 064
3.	C 40 035	Z 14 035	7.	P 50 025	T 15 025
4.	Y 80 067	I 18 067	8.	E 60 302	A 16 302

Using Math and Reading a Paycheck Stub

(reading and understanding a paycheck stub; adding, subtracting, and multiplying decimals)

Every paycheck from the Thrifty Department Store has two parts, the check and the stub. The stub shows:

1. the *hours* you work
2. the *gross pay* (the amount of money you make)
3. the *deductions* (the money that comes out of your check) and
4. the *net pay* (the money you make after the deductions).

Here are some deductions on a paycheck stub.
FICA is the amount that comes out for Social Security taxes.
Federal is the amount that comes out for federal taxes to the United States.
State is the amount that comes out for state taxes to the state where you live.
Ins. is the amount that comes out for medical insurance.

Read Eva's paycheck stub.

Thrifty Department Store
2028 West North Avenue Phoenix, AZ

Employee's Name	Social Security Number	Rate	Period Ending	Check Number
Canseco, Eva	341-52-5153	5.00	05-20-93	81057

Earnings	Hours	Current	Year to Date	Deductions	Current	Year to Date
Gross Pay	40.00	200.00	3,800.00	FICA	8.00	152.00
				Federal	20.25	384.75
				State	7.17	136.23
				Ins.	20.00	380.00
				Total Deductions	55.42	1052.98
				Net Pay	144.48	2745.12

Read Eva's paycheck stub. Answer the questions. Write on the lines.

1. How much money does Eva make per hour? ____________
2. What is Eva's gross pay for this paycheck? ____________
3. How much does Eva pay for Social Security (FICA) for this pay period?

   ____
4. How much does Eva pay for federal taxes for this pay period? ____________
5. How much does Eva pay for state taxes for this pay period? ____________
6. How much does Eva pay for insurance for this pay period? ____________
7. What is Eva's net pay for this pay period? ____________
8. Eva receives a raise of .50 per hour. What is her new rate? ____________
9. If Eva works 40 hours at the new rate, what is her gross pay? ____________
10. Eva pays $8.15 for FICA, $21.06 for federal taxes, $7.97 for state taxes, and $21.00 for insurance. What are Eva's total deductions? ____________
11. What is Eva's new net pay? (*Hint:* New gross pay – new deductions = new net pay) ____________

UNIT 9 *Goal Setting*

Before You Read

(making predictions, relating experiences to reading, establishing prior knowledge)

Look at the picture.

Talk about the picture with a partner.

Read the questions.

Write the answers on the lines.

1. Where is the employee in the picture? ______________________
2. What is he thinking about? ______________________
3. When you think about your future, what things do you want to do? ________

____

Reading About Work

Gilberto Sets Goals

Gilberto is a patient transporter at the hospital. He takes the patients to the X-ray department or to the laboratory for the tests they need. Then he brings the patients back to their rooms.

Gilberto likes the patients. The patients like Gilberto, too. He helps them feel more comfortable and less nervous.

Right now Gilberto is on break in the cafeteria. He is thinking about his future. He wants to stay at the hospital, but he needs to make more money. His rent is going up, his car needs repairs, and he wants to get married next year.

"I need to set some goals," says Gilberto to himself. "I need more money, but I like working here. I need a different job, one that makes more money."

Just then, Gilberto's friend, Leroy, walks into the cafeteria.

"That's it," Gilberto says softly. "I'll talk to Leroy. He's a laboratory technician. He works with patients. He makes more money than I make. He works weekdays and day-shift hours, not the crazy days and hours I sometimes get. Hey, Leroy, wait a minute. I want to talk to you."

"Are you going to buy my lunch, old buddy?" Leroy jokes. "Not today. I'm saving my money for school," Gilberto says.

"For school?" Leroy asks.

"That's what I want to talk to you about," Gilberto begins. "And I have a million questions."

Understanding New Words

(expanding vocabulary, understanding and using new words)

A. Work with a partner. Read the words in the box. Find and circle the words in the story on page 84.

patients	future	goals	weekday	million

B. Take turns reading these sentences and the words below with a partner. Decide together how to finish each sentence. Write the words on the lines.

1. Gilberto thinks about the *future.* The *future* is the time ____________________ ______________________________.
   - that will be tomorrow, next week, or next year.
   - that was yesterday.
   - that is right now.
2. "I need to set some *goals,*" says Gilberto. *Goals* are things you ______________ ______________________________.
   - want to eat right now.
   - want to do in the future.
   - want to wear tomorrow.
3. A hospital has many *patients. Patients* are people who __________________.
   - visit the hospital.
   - work in the hospital.
   - are sick.
4. Leroy works *weekdays.* He works on ______________________________ ____.
   - Monday, Tuesday, Wednesday, Thursday, and Friday.
   - Friday, Saturday, and Sunday.
   - holidays, Saturday, and Sunday.
5. Gilberto has a *million* questions. The number for one million is ____________.
   - 10,000
   - 1,000,000
   - 100,000

Understanding the Reading

(checking literal comprehension)

Read these sentences with your partner. One word in each sentence is wrong. Correct each sentence with your partner. Write the new sentence on the line.

1. Gilberto takes the equipment to the X-ray department.

    ____

2. Gilberto is on break in the hospital lobby.

    ____

3. Gilberto needs to set some tables for his future.

    ____

4. A laboratory technician works weekend hours.

    ____

5. Gilberto wants to get married next month.

    ____

6. Leroy wants Gilberto to buy him dinner.

    ____

7. Gilberto is saving his money for a vacation.

    ____

Discussing

Activity #1 *(distinguishing facts and opinions)*

Take turns reading these sentences with a partner. Is each sentence a **fact** (something you can prove) or an **opinion** (something you believe is true)? Decide with your partner. Put a check (✔) under **Fact** or **Opinion**.

	Fact	Opinion
1. Gilberto has an important job in the hospital.	________	________
2. The cafeteria food doesn't taste very good.	________	________
3. Gilberto's friend is a laboratory technician.	________	________
4. A person goes to school to be a laboratory technician.	________	________
5. Setting goals for the future is important.	________	________
6. There are 29 classes a student takes to become a laboratory technician.	________	________
7. Laboratory technicians work weekday hours.	________	________
8. Classes for laboratory technicians are too expensive.	________	________

Activity #2 *(using creative thinking skills in role plays, empathizing with a character)*

Work with a partner. Act out what happens.

Student A is an employee who wants to get a promotion to a higher job in the company. Student B is the supervisor. The employee asks the supervisor what to do to get a promotion. The supervisor thinks the employee is a hard worker and a good candidate for a promotion. The supervisor gives the employee some ideas to help get a promotion.

Activity #3 *(prioritizing goals)*

Read the personal goals. Put the goals in order from 1 to 5. Use 1 for the goal that is most important to you. Use 5 for the goal that is least important to you. Do the same for the work goals.

Personal goals

____ Lose ten pounds.

____ Buy a new car.

____ Save more money.

____ Spend more time with my family.

____ Learn more English.

Work goals

____ Win an employee award.

____ Finish my work faster.

____ Come on time every day.

____ Do not make mistakes in my work.

____ Get a promotion to a higher job.

Now discuss these questions with your partner. Share your answers with the class.

1. What personal goal is most important to you? (number 1)
2. What personal goal is least important to you? (number 5)
3. What work goal is most important to you? (number 1)
4. What work goal is least important to you? (number 5)
5. What other personal or work goals do you have that are not on the list?

Reading at Work

Understanding New Words

(expanding vocabulary, understanding and using new words and phrases)

Read the sentences below. Find and circle the underlined words in the following reading.

1. There is a job open in the laboratory. The position is for a lab technician.
2. Gilberto worked three years as a patient transporter. He has three years' experience in his job.
3. Elmwood Park Hospital wants its lab technicians to have 3–5 years experience in a hospital laboratory and a degree in Medical Laboratory Technology. The experience and the schooling are the qualifications a person needs for this job.
4. Medical insurance pays for the hospital and the doctor when an employee is sick. The company pays part of the insurance. The employee pays the other part of the insurance.
5. The salary range for this job is $13,000–$15,000. The lowest salary for this job is $13,000. The highest salary is $15,000.

Some companies put job openings on an employee bulletin board. Read the job opening for a Laboratory Technician below.

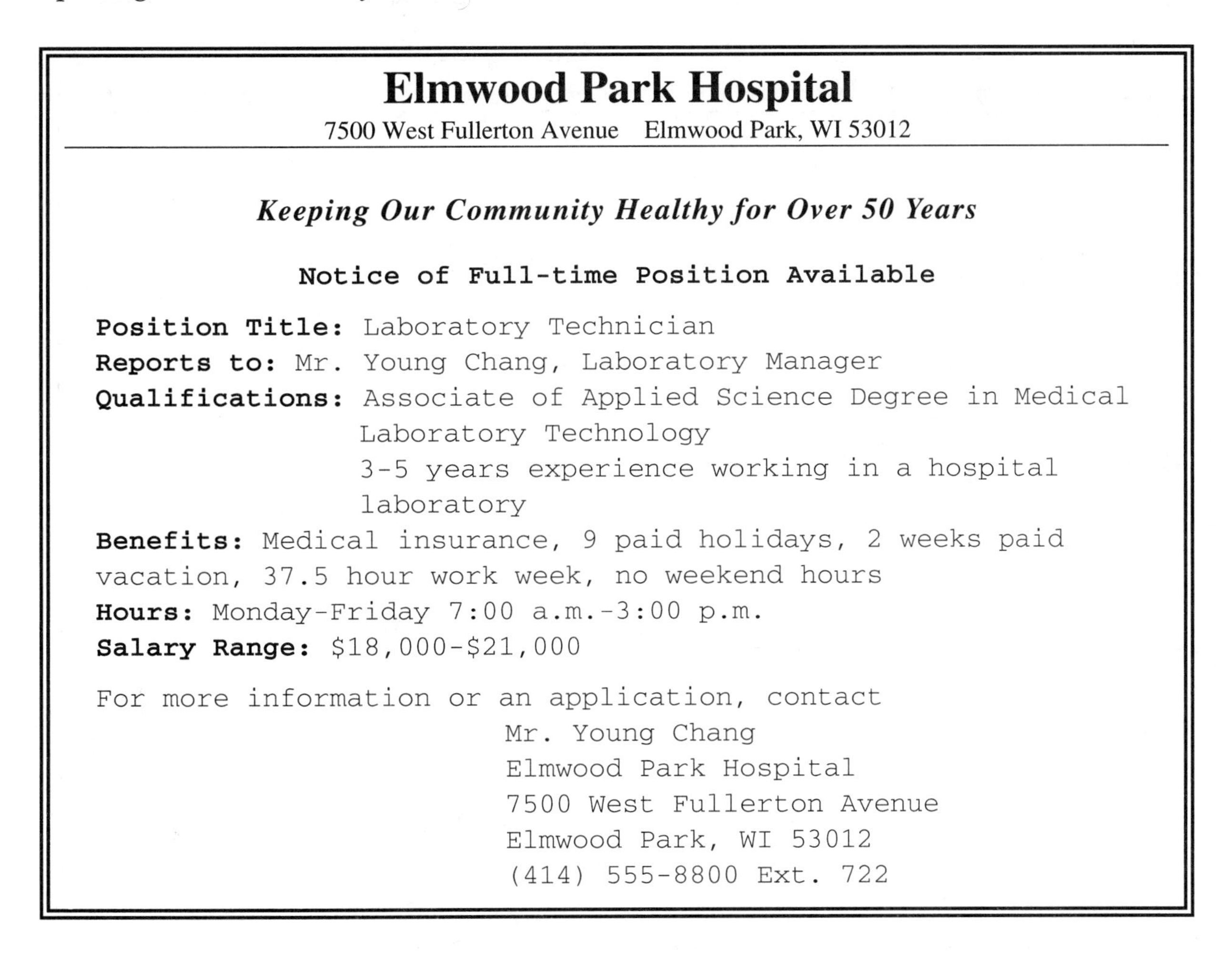

Elmwood Park Hospital

7500 West Fullerton Avenue Elmwood Park, WI 53012

Keeping Our Community Healthy for Over 50 Years

Notice of Full-time Position Available

Position Title: Laboratory Technician
Reports to: Mr. Young Chang, Laboratory Manager
Qualifications: Associate of Applied Science Degree in Medical Laboratory Technology
3-5 years experience working in a hospital laboratory
Benefits: Medical insurance, 9 paid holidays, 2 weeks paid vacation, 37.5 hour work week, no weekend hours
Hours: Monday-Friday 7:00 a.m.-3:00 p.m.
Salary Range: $18,000-$21,000

For more information or an application, contact
Mr. Young Chang
Elmwood Park Hospital
7500 West Fullerton Avenue
Elmwood Park, WI 53012
(414) 555-8800 Ext. 722

Understanding the Reading

(checking literal comprehension, comparing and contrasting actual experiences with reading)

Answer the questions. Write on the lines.

1. What job is open at the hospital? ____________________
2. What are the qualifications for this job? ____________________

   ____
3. What is the salary range for this job? ____________________
4. Think about your job and this job opening. What benefits are the same?

   ____

   What benefits are different? ____________________

Writing

(relating reading to job experiences, writing pertinent job information)

Complete the form with information for your job.

Position Title: ____________________

Reports to: ____________________

Qualifications: ____________________

____

Benefits: ____________________

____

Hours: ____________________

Salary Range: ____________________

Listening

Activity #1 *(listening for specific information)*

Listen to the tape of the hospital employees. Put a check (✔) for each goal the employees have.

	Gilberto	Leroy	Kim	Jenna
1. eat more fruits and vegetables				
2. make more money				
3. save more money				
4. get a promotion				
5. buy a new car				
6. take a laboratory technology class				
7. win Employee of the Year award				
8. exercise for 15 minutes every day				
9. lose 10 pounds				
10. have more free time				
11. learn to use a computer				
12. learn to speak more English				
13. travel to a foreign country				
14. take a math class				

Activity # 2 *(listening for specific information)*

Listen to the tape. Circle the correct information.

1. *Position Title:* Nursing Assistant Patient Transporter X-ray Technician
2. *Reports to:* Mrs. Olivia Armstrong Mr. Otto Anderson Ms. Alice Osterman
3. *Experience Needed:* 2 years 3 years 4 years 5 years
4. *Paid holidays:* 8 9 10 11
5. *Weeks of paid vacation:* 1 week 2 weeks 3 weeks
6. *Hours:* 6:30–2:30 7:00–3:00 8:00–4:00 8:30–4:30
7. *Salary:* $15,000 $18,000 $21,000

Using Math

(solving problems using multiplication and division)

Many people save money for different reasons. They save money every week or every month to meet their goals.

Read the problems. Circle *multiply* or *divide.* Solve the problems.

1.	Gilberto needs $750 for school. He saves $50 every week. How many weeks will it take Gilberto to save the money? _______ weeks	*multiply*	*divide*
2.	Gilberto plans to take five classes. Books for each class cost about $18.00. How much will Gilberto spend on books for his classes? ___________	*multiply*	*divide*
3.	Diana wants to take a vacation in six months. She needs $600 for the trip. How much does she need to save every month? ___________ How much does she need to save every week? (*Hint:* There are 4 weeks in one month.) ________	*multiply*	*divide*
4.	Tina needs a new car. She has $3,000 now. She needs $2,600 more for the car she wants. How much money does she need to save every week if she wants to buy the car in four months? __________ every week	*multiply*	*divide*
5.	Bill got a promotion. He takes home an extra $22.50 a week. He decides to save this money. How much will he have in one year? (*Hint:* One year is 52 weeks.) __________	*multiply*	*divide*

UNIT 10 *Job Training/Continuing Education*

Before You Read

(making predictions, relating experiences to reading, establishing prior knowledge)

Reprinted with special permission of King Features Syndicate, Inc.

Look at the cartoon.

Talk about the cartoon with a partner.

Read the questions.

Write the answers on the lines.

1. What is Hagar the Horrible saying? ______________________________

   ____

2. Why does the employee hate on the job training? ____________________
3. What training did you get at work to do your job? ___________________
4. Who trained you for your job? _________________________________

Reading About Work

Clara's Computer Classes

Clara and her supervisor, Mrs. McKay, are talking about the new computers the factory will begin to use. Clara looks nervous and pale.

CLARA: Mrs. McKay, don't you think the people here at Rainbow Paints are good workers?

MRS. MCKAY: Why, yes, Clara. All the people I supervise are excellent employees, hard-working and responsible. And I know our profits are increasing. The president is delighted about that.

CLARA: Well, then why do we need those new computers? We can do our jobs without them. You and the president are friends. Please talk to him. Ask him to change his mind about buying the computers.

MRS. MCKAY: Clara, why are you so upset about the new computers?

CLARA: Because I don't know how to use a computer. What if I make a mistake? What if I break the computer? Will you fire me?

MRS. MCKAY: Of course not, Clara. Right now no one knows how to use the new computers. But all the employees will learn—you, me, even the president. The computer company is sending an instructor here to teach us. We'll have classes next week in the lunch room. Some of the computers are there already.

CLARA: I feel a little better now. I can continue to work here and also learn something new.

MRS. MCKAY: That's right, Clara. And with computers, we can work faster and make fewer mistakes. Think of the computer as a new friend.

CLARA: Okay, Mrs. McKay. Let's go to the lunch room and say hello to our "new friends."

Understanding New Words

(expanding vocabulary, using and understanding new words and phrases)

A. Work with a partner. Read the words in the box. Find and circle the words in the story on page 94.

pale	delighted	change his mind	fire	instructor

B. Take turns reading these sentences and the words below with a partner. Decide together how to finish each sentence. Write the words on the lines.

1. When the profits increase, the president is *delighted. Delighted* means ________________________.

   full of light.
   very, very happy.
   rich.

2. "I will *fire* any employee who uses drugs on the job," said the supervisor. To *fire* is to ______________________________.

   tell not to come back to work.
   come back in a week.
   give an award.

3. Margaret doesn't want to work overtime. Then she *changes her mind.* Margaret ______________________________.

   decides not to work overtime.
   decides to work overtime.
   decides to get a different job.

4. An *instructor* teaches a class or a group of people. An *instructor* is a ____________________.

   supervisor.
   candidate.
   teacher.

5. An employee is sick. His head hurts, and his face is *pale. Pale* skin is ______________________.

   a very light color.
   a very dark color.
   a red color.

Understanding the Reading

(checking literal and inferential comprehension)

Fill in the circle that answers the question.

1. Who is Mrs. McKay?
   - ❍ Clara's supervisor at Rainbow Paints
   - ❍ the president's wife
   - ❍ the computer instructor

2. Why is Clara nervous and pale?
   - ❍ She is getting married
   - ❍ She is upset about using the new computers
   - ❍ She is getting sick

3. Who knows how to use the new computers at Rainbow Paints?
   - ❍ only the president
   - ❍ Mrs. McKay
   - ❍ no one

4. Why are the computer classes in the lunchroom?
   - ❍ because it is a large room that is empty some of the time
   - ❍ because the employees are hungry during the classes
   - ❍ because it is close to the president's office

5. Why does Clara feel better at the end of the story?
   - ❍ because she likes her supervisor
   - ❍ because Mrs. McKay will not fire her if she makes a mistake on the computer
   - ❍ because she knows how to use a computer

Discussing

Activity #1 *(distinguishing facts and opinions)*

Take turns reading these sentences with a partner. Is each sentence a *fact* (something you can prove) or an *opinion* (something you believe is true)? Decide with your partner. Put a check (✔) under *Fact* or *Opinion*.

	Fact	**Opinion**
1. Some employees receive on-the-job training.	______	______
2. The best person to train new employees is the supervisor.	______	______
3. People over 50 years old are too old to learn about computers.	______	______
4. The best time to train an employee is in the morning.	______	______
5. Computers are used in many companies.	______	______
6. Computers are difficult to operate.	______	______

Activity #2 *(using creative thinking skills in role plays, empathizing with a character)*

Work with a group of three students. Act out what happens.

1. Student A is the boss. The boss explains to Students B and C that they need to take a computer class at the company.
   Student B agrees but is nervous about taking the class.
   Student C disagrees and does not want to take any class.

2. Student B is the instructor of the company's math class.
   Student C enjoys the class but doesn't have time to do any homework for the class.
   Student A does all the homework but doesn't understand the instructor.

Activity #3 *(relating reading to life experiences, making predictions)*

Now discuss these questions with your group. Share your answers with the class.

1. What kind of job training did you receive for your job?
2. When did you receive your job training?
3. Do you continue to learn at work? What do you learn?
4. What will you need to learn in the next year?
5. What will you need to learn in the next five years?

Reading at Work

Understanding New Words

(expanding vocabulary, understanding and using words in context)

Read the sentences below. Find and circle the underlined words in the reading.

1. "In conjunction with" means "together with." The company president, in conjunction with the supervisors, decides on the date for the company picnic.
2. An instructor is a teacher. Mrs. Byrne is the instructor for the writing class. She teaches the writing class.
3. Every employee is compensated for his or her work. Every employee receives pay for his or her work.
4. Anne is purchasing books for her math class. She is buying her books from the bookstore.
5. Students complete forms with personal information to register for a class.

Many companies use memos like the one below to communicate with their employees. Read the memo to the employees of Rainbow Paints.

Rainbow Paints

4568 Western Avenue Santa Clara, CA 95052 555–1020

To: All Employees
From: Mark Schulz, Human Resources Manager
Date: October 20, 1992
Re: Workplace Classes

Rainbow Paints, in conjunction with Harper University, will offer two classes for employees who wish to improve their writing or math skills.

Effective Writing will be offered on Tuesdays from 3:45-5:45 P.M. from November 3, 1992 to January 26, 1993. Improving Basic Skills in Mathematics will be offered on Thursdays from 3:45-5:45 P.M. from November 5, 1992 to January 28, 1993. Instructors from Harper University will teach the classes in the lunchroom.

Employees will be compensated at their regular rate for the first hour of the class. The second hour of class will be the employees' personal time. Employees are responsible for purchasing their own books. Books will be available in the lunch room on the first day of class.

Interested employees should come to the Human Resources Office to register for classes.

Understanding the Reading

(checking literal comprehension, using vocabulary in context)

Complete the sentences.

The memo is for ________________________. The memo is about or regarding _________________ _____________. Rainbow Paints, in ________________ with Harper University, will offer _____ classes for employees. The writing class will be on _________________ from _________ to ___________. The math class will be on ________________ from ________ to ________. Employees will be ________________ for the first hour of class. Employees are responsible for __________________ their own books for the classes. An interested employee should come to the Human Resources Office to _____________ for a class.

Writing

(completing a form, giving reasons for actions)

Fill in the information to register for a class. The class will be at the workplace.

Social Security Number ________-____-________ Date _______________
month/day/year

Name: ____
last first middle

Address: ______________________________ ______________________
street city state zip code

Telephone Number: _(____)________________ __(____)________________
work home

Department: __________________________ Supervisor:________________

Reasons for taking the class:

I want to take _____________________ because ________________________

____

____.

I understand that I will be compensated for the first hour of class. I also understand that the second hour of class will be my own personal time. I agree to purchase the required books for the class.

____
Employee's signature

Listening

Activity #1 *(Listening for specific information)*

Listen to the tape of the conversation. Circle the words to complete the sentences.

1. Clara is reading

    her favorite magazine.
    the company newsletter.
    the directions to operate the computer.

2. "Painting the Town" is

    the name of the company newsletter.
    the name of Clara's favorite nightclub.
    the name of the company cafeteria.

3. Joe started working at Rainbow Paints

    three years ago.
    three months ago.
    three weeks ago.

4. At the beginning of the conversation, Joe believes

    that computers are difficult to use.
    that learning and school are for kids.
    that the company newsletter is interesting.

5. Think of your training time as

    a time to relax on the job.
    the first day at work.
    learning while you earn.

6. Employees at Rainbow Paints will keep track of orders, production, and supplies with

    calendars.
    computers.
    schedules.

7. The next copy of "Painting the Town"

    will be done on a computer.
    will be ready in one month.
    will be about vacations.

8. An instructor from CompuTech, the computer company, will be at Rainbow Paints for

   the next two weeks.
   the next two months.
   the next two days.

9. The instructor will give each supervisor

   a computer to practice on at home.
   a computer manual to study.
   a schedule for the classes.

10. Employees who want more time to practice using the computers may

    take another computer class at Harper University.
    come to the lunch room before or after their shift.
    ask the instructor questions after their classes.

11. If the company's profits decrease,

    the employees can lose their jobs.
    the employees can work overtime.
    the employees can have long vacations.

12. Joe's son and daughter are learning to use computers

    to play video games.
    in their jobs.
    at school.

13. Joe is

    14 years old.
    40 years old.
    44 years old.

Using Math and a Pie Chart

(reading and interpreting a pie chart, multiplying by decimals, translating information from a pie chart to a bar graph)

Harper University uses a pie chart to show the nationalities (the countries where the students come from) of international students who attend the school. The pie chart is a circle. The complete circle is 100%. Each part of the circle is less than 100%. Add all the parts of the pie chart together to make 100%.

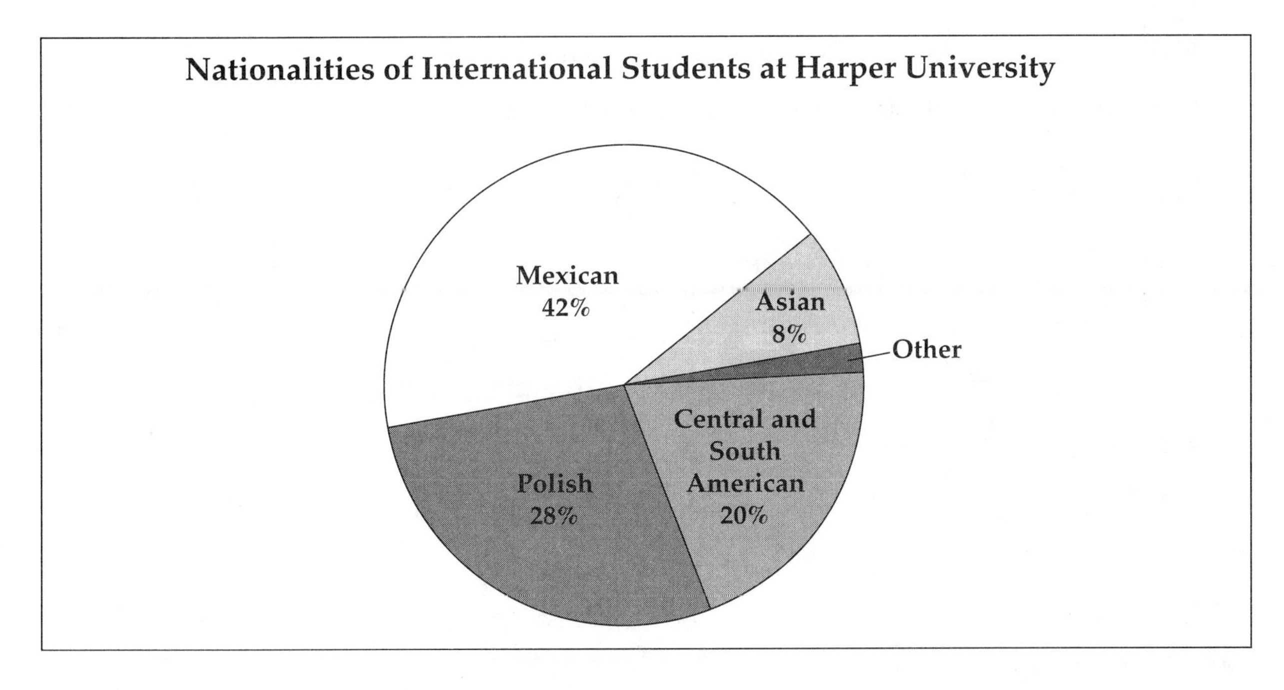

A. Use the pie chart to answer the questions. Write the answers on the lines.

1. What percentage of students are Mexicans? ___________
2. What percentage of students are Asian? __________
3. What percentage of students are Central and South American? __________
4. What percentage of students are Polish? __________
5. What percentage of students are not Mexican, Asian, Polish, or Central or South American? __________
6. What percentage of students equal one half (50%) of the number of international students? ____________________
7. What percentage of international students are not Mexican? _________

If you know the total number of international students and the percentage from one country, you can figure out the exact number of students from one country. Harper University has 1500 international students: 42% are Mexican.

```
  1500  = the total number of international students
 X .42  = the percentage of Mexican students (42 %)
 -----
  3000
 6000
 -----
630.00  (Remember to count 2 decimal places in your answer.)
```

There are 630 Mexican students at Harper University.

B. Change the percent to a decimal. Multiply and write the answers.

1. How many students are Mexican? ________________
2. How many students are Asian? ________________
3. How many students are Central and South American? ________________
4. How many students are Polish? ________________
5. How many students are not Mexican, Asian, Polish, or Central or South American? ________________

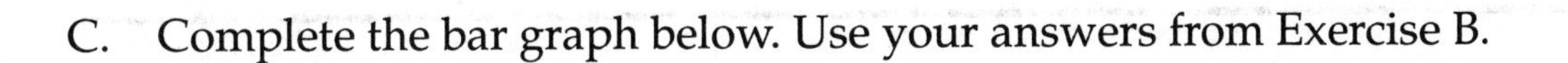

C. Complete the bar graph below. Use your answers from Exercise B.

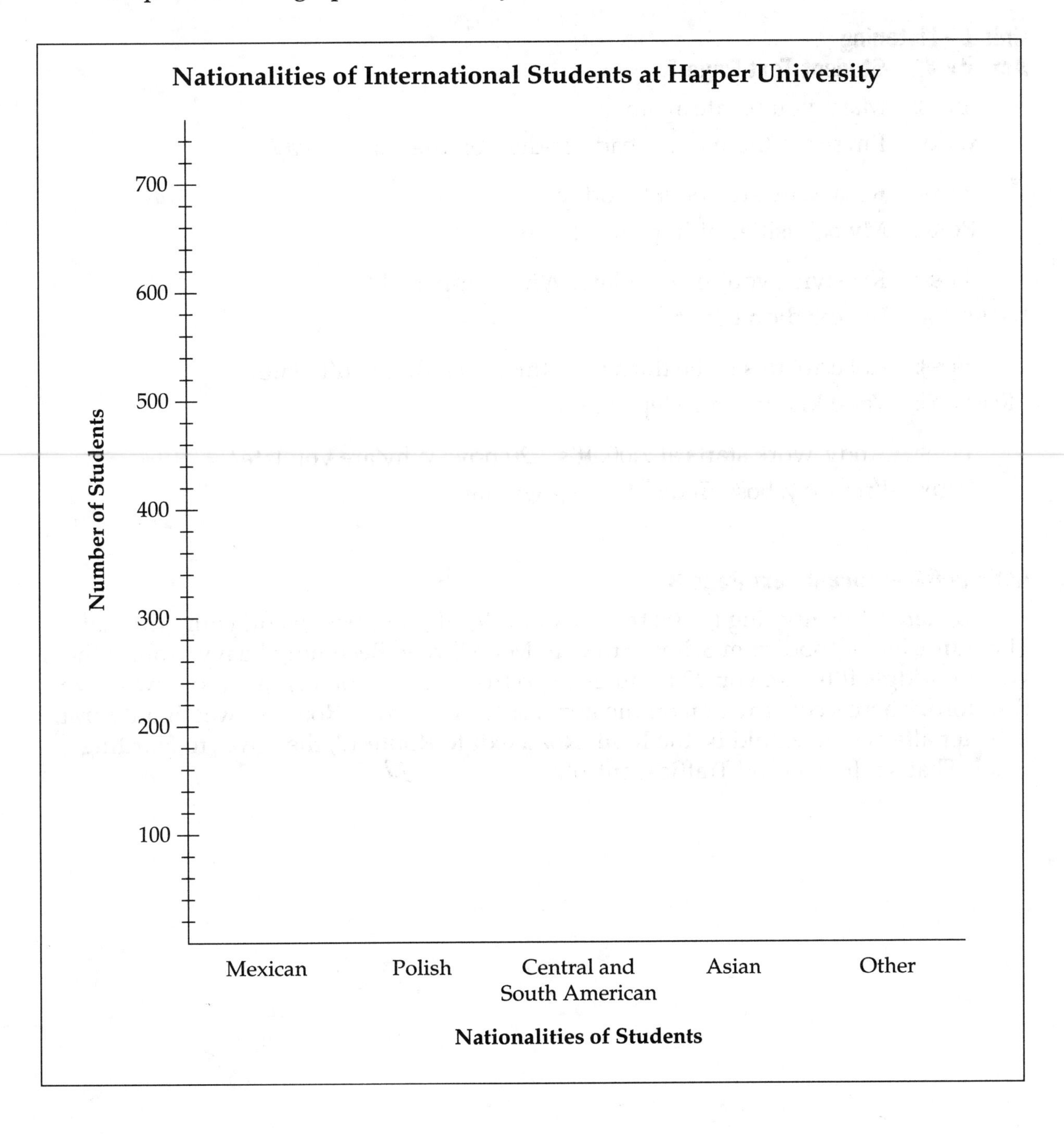

Unit 1—Listening
Activity #1—Student Text Page 7

BOSS: Mary, you're late again.
MARY: I'm sorry, there was a bad accident on the expressway.

BOSS: Rosa, why are you late today?
ROSA: My babysitter didn't come today.

BOSS: Krystyna, you're never late. What happened?
KRYSTYNA: My car didn't start.

BOSS: Roberto, this is the third time this week that you're late!
ROBERTO: Yes, I know. I overslept again.

BOSS: Andy, work starts at 7:00. It's 7:20 now. Why are you late?
ANDY: I'm sorry, boss. Today the bus was late.

Activity #2—Student Text Page 8

Well, here's the morning traffic from station WESL, number 990 on your AM dial. The traffic looks good from School Street to Main Street. Becoming heavy around the Wilson Bridge. It'll take you 20 minutes to go from the Wilson Bridge into downtown Rockford. There's construction on the north side of Harding Road, so watch out for it. A better alternative would be the River Road exit to Route 17, then over to Harding Road. That's it for Central Traffic Control.

Unit 2—Listening
Activity #1—Student Text Page 16

CUSTOMER A: I'll have the baked chicken with pineapple, please.
WAITER: That comes with a salad. What kind of salad dressing do you want?
CUSTOMER A: French dressing, please.
WAITER: Do you want a baked potato, mashed potato, french fries, or rice?
CUSTOMER A: I'll take the baked potato.
WAITER: Our vegetables are green beans, carrots, peas, or corn.
CUSTOMER A: Corn sounds good.
WAITER: Can I bring you another Coke®?
CUSTOMER A: No, but I do like coffee after dinner.
WAITER: Thank you. I'll be right back with your salad.

CUSTOMER B: How is the shrimp today? Is it fresh?
WAITRESS: Yes, it's very fresh and delicious. I recommend it.
CUSTOMER B: OK, I'll have the shrimp and rice.
WAITRESS: Your dinner comes with a salad. What kind of dressing do you want?
CUSTOMER B: I don't want a salad tonight, thank you.
WAITRESS: Fine. How about green beans, carrots, peas, or corn?
CUSTOMER B: I love green beans.
WAITRESS: Do you want coffee or tea with your dinner or after your dinner?
CUSTOMER B: I think I'll have some tea with my dinner. Can I order dessert now?
WAITRESS: Sure. We have apple or cherry pie, chocolate cake, or fortune cookies.
CUSTOMER B: I'll have the fortune cookies.
WAITRESS: Great. I'll bring you some hot tea right now.

WAITRESS: Hello. May I get you a drink?
CUSTOMER C: Sure. I'll have some milk.
WAITRESS: Are you ready to order you dinner?
Customer C: Yes. The steak looks good.
WAITRESS: Do you want it cooked rare, medium, or well done?
CUSTOMER C: Medium, please.
WAITRESS: Baked potato, mashed potato, french fries, or rice?
CUSTOMER C: I prefer french fries.
WAITRESS: Corn, peas, green beans, or carrots?
CUSTOMER C: Carrots, please, if they are fresh.
WAITRESS: Yes, they are.
CUSTOMER C: And I'd like some chocolate cake for dessert, too.
WAITRESS: Coming right up!

Activity #2—Student Text Page 17

1. Today all the customers want fresh shrimp. They love the way I cook it!
2. Daddy, can I have some chocolate cake after dinner?
3. Hello. My name is Gina. Are you ready to order?

Unit 3—Listening
Activity #1—Student Text Page 29

Good morning, ladies and gentlemen, and welcome to Security Airlines Flight 2028. You will notice the emergency exits at the sides of the airplane. In an emergency landing, these exits will open to allow passengers to leave the plane. Your seat cushion becomes a flotation device in water. This is your oxygen mask. To use the mask, simply place it over your nose and mouth and breathe normally. Overhead is the seat belt sign. During takeoff and landing, your seats must be in the upright position. Please keep seat belts fastened until the captain turns off the "Fasten Seat Belts" sign. Thank you and have a pleasant flight.

Activity #2—Student Text Page 30

1. May I have your attention, please. Eagle Airlines Flight 550 for Chicago is now boarding at Gate 17A.
2. Attention, please. Passengers may now board Swift Airlines Flight number 1020 at Gate 8B. This flight will depart for Los Angeles at 12:19 p.m.
3. Good afternoon, ladies and gentlemen. Passengers for Sky High Airlines Flight 810, departing at 2:30 for New York, may now board at Gate 12C.
4. Your attention, please. Passengers for Skyhoppers Airlines Commuter Flight 412 to Omaha, Nebraska are now boarding at Gate 11A. Flight 412 will depart at 3:45 p.m. Thank you.

Unit 4—Listening
Activity #1—Student Text Page 40

CARMEN: Hi, Lillian. How are you today?

LILLIAN: I'm fine, Carmen. How are you?

CARMEN: Great. Thank you. Do you know that today is the 10th anniversary of Freddy's Finest Foods? We are having a special sale. The cashiers use the sale prices only for today.

LILLIAN: I didn't know that, Carmen. How many things are on sale today?

CARMEN: There are 10 things on sale.

Porterhouse steak is $3.99 a pound.

Freddy's Frozen Orange Juice is 99¢ for a 12-ounce can.

Sweet corn is 12¢ an ear.

Red potatoes are 10¢ a pound.

Green or red grapes are 98¢ a pound.

Wake Up Coffee is $3.79 for a 26-ounce can.

Thirsty Paper Towels are 89¢ a roll.

Fresh and Tasty Turkey is $1.30 a pound.

So Soft Toilet Tissue is $1.19 for a 4-roll package.

Country Fresh Cottage Cheese is $1.69 for a 24-ounce container.

LILLIAN: Carmen, can you repeat those prices? I want to write them down so I will remember them.

CARMEN: You don't need to write the prices down, Lillian. Every time Freddy's Finest Foods has a sale, the cashiers get a list of the sale prices. The list is at your register. You can look at the list for the sale prices. Just try to remember the things on sale.

LILLIAN: Thanks, Carmen. I **will** look at the list. I'm glad you are here to help me.

CARMEN: It's no problem. After a couple of weeks, you won't need any help. And don't worry. You're doing fine. See you at lunchtime.

LILLIAN: Great. I'm already hungry.

Unit 5—Listening
Activities #1 and #2—Student Text Page 50

SWITCHBOARD OPERATOR: Hello. Sleepy Hollow Hotel. May I help you?

CUSTOMER: Yes. I'd like some information about your hotel services and your prices, please.

SWITCHBOARD OPERATOR: Thank you. I'll connect you with Ms. DeCarlo, our customer service representative.

CUSTOMER: Thank you.

THERESA DECARLO: Sleepy Hollow Hotel. Theresa DeCarlo speaking.

CUSTOMER: Hello. I'd like some information about your hotel services and your prices, please.

THERESA DECARLO: Of course. We have a beautiful hotel in downtown Chicago. Price for a single room, with one double bed is $55.00 per night. Price for a double room with two double beds is $70.00 per night. Every room has a color TV. Cable television channels are available for $4.00 per day. Every room also has an AM/FM radio and is air-conditioned for your comfort. Parking is available in our underground parking lot. Our parking attendants will park your car for you. We have an indoor swimming pool, a video-game room, an exercise room, and several conference rooms for business meetings.

CUSTOMER: Do you have any restaurants in the hotel?

THERESA DECARLO: I'm glad you asked. The Sleepy Hollow Snack Shop is our coffee shop, open for breakfast, lunch, and snacks. Our more formal restaurant, The Legend, is open every evening for dinner and also on Sundays for brunch from 10:00 until 2:00. You can order room service 24-hours a day.

CUSTOMER: Do you have babysitters for the children?

THERESA DECARLO: Yes. You can arrange for a babysitter at the front desk in the lobby. The charge is $3.00 an hour for one child or $4.00 an hour for two or more children. This is a nice service, especially if you want to enjoy a late, romantic dinner at The Legend.

CUSTOMER: Thank you. It sounds very nice.

THERESA DECARLO: You're welcome. Our reservation clerk can take your reservation whenever you are ready.

BRENDA: Hello. Budget Quality Motel. Brenda speaking.

CUSTOMER: Hello. I'd like some information about your hotel services and your prices, please.

BRENDA: Sure. Our single room rate is $25.00 per night. Our double room rate is $35.00 per night. All our rooms are air-conditioned. There is a TV and an AM/FM radio in every room.

CUSTOMER: Do you have cable television channels?

BRENDA: No, I'm sorry.

CUSTOMER: How about a swimming pool?

BRENDA: No, we don't have a swimming pool. We do have a few video games.

CUSTOMER: Do you have any restaurants?

BRENDA: Yes, we have one family restaurant, the Dollar Stretcher Diner. Children under 4 years old eat free.

CUSTOMER: That sounds great. Is room service available?

BRENDA: No, Ma'am. We have vending machines in the motel lobby if you get hungry after the diner closes.

CUSTOMER: Do you have babysitters for the children?

BRENDA: No, Ma'am.

CUSTOMER: How about parking services?

BRENDA: Well, we have a large parking lot in front of the motel.

CUSTOMER: Thank you very much.

BRENDA: You're welcome.

Unit 6—Listening Activity—Student Text Page 59

NARRATOR: Number one.

MR. MORTON: Harry, there's a problem with this circuit board.

NARRATOR: Number two.

MRS. PERRY: Emily, I want to talk to you. Can you come to my office, please?

NARRATOR: Number three.

MR. LENNON: Salvatore, do you understand how to load this machine?

NARRATOR: Number four.

MS. BRENNAN: I want you to come back from break after 15 minutes, Wanda. Do not take a break for longer than 15 minutes.

NARRATOR: Number five.

PERSONNEL MANAGER: If you take Friday off, Nick, you won't get paid for the holiday on Thursday. That's the company's policy.

NARRATOR: Number six.

CO-WORKER: I can't find the ladder, Eduardo. I think you put it away in the wrong place.

NARRATOR: Number seven.

CO-WORKER: Hey, Abdul, you can't smoke here. This is a non-smoking area. If you want to smoke you have to go to the cafeteria.

NARRATOR: Number eight.

ROSEMARY: Marilyn, here's another product with a defect. I want you to check every box carefully.

Unit 7—Listening
Activity #1—Student Text Page 69

Good morning, supervisors. I want to talk to you about a new company program. We all want to encourage our excellent employees to continue to do a good job. We want the other employees to see that we think it is important to have dependable and responsible workers. I now have a program to reward the best employees. It is the Employee of the Month Program.

Every month, you, the supervisors, can recommend one of your employees. Choose an employee who has good attendance, comes on time, works especially hard, and gets along well with co-workers. Fill out the recommendation form in the Personnel Office.

I will read all the recommendations and choose one winner each month. The winner will receive a bonus of $50.00. In December, the names of the monthly winners will go into a hat. I will pick out one name. That employee will be the Employee of the Year. The Employee of the Year will receive two extra paid vacation days and a bonus of $250.00.

Unit 8—Listening
Activity #1—Student Text Page 80

CASHIER: Attention, a clerk from audio/video. I need a price check on Hollywood Videotapes. 3 pack. That's Hollywood Videotapes in a 3 pack for register 10.

AUDIO/VISUAL CLERK: Register 10. Here's the price you wanted on the Hollywood Videotapes. A 3 pack is on sale for $5.99. That's $5.99 for a 3 pack of Hollywood Videotapes.

CASHIER: Will a clerk from domestics please call register 7? A clerk from domestics call register 7.

DOMESTICS CLERK: Hi, I'm from domestics. How can I help you?

CASHIER: I need a price check on a Quick 'n Clean Broom.

DOMESTICS CLERK: OK, I'll check. That's $3.79 for a Quick 'n Clean Broom. $3.79.

CASHIER: Thanks.

CASHIER: I need a price check from the pharmacy, please. Register 16 needs a price check from the pharmacy on Energy Plus Daily Vitamins, 100 tablets.

PHARMACY CLERK: Pharmacy here. What's the item?

CASHIER: It's Energy Plus Daily Vitamins, 100 tablets.

PHARMACY: Regular or Extra Strength.

CASHIER: Just the regular.

PHARMACY CLERK: OK, that's $4.15. $4.15 for 100 tablets.

CASHIER: This is register 2. I need a price check from electronics, please. Will a clerk from electronics please call register 2 for a price check?

ELECTRONICS CLERK: Hi, this is electronics. What do you need?

CASHIER: I need the price on the Phone Friend Answering Machine.

ELECTRONICS CLERK: Is that the one with the telephone and answering machine together?

CASHIER: No, it's only the answering machine.

ELECTRONICS CLERK: OK. That's on sale until Wednesday for $52.99.

CASHIER: $52.99? OK, thanks a lot.

CASHIER: Will a clerk from Home and Garden please call register 4? That's a clerk from Home and Garden, call register 4 for a price check on a 33-gallon trash can.

HOME AND GARDEN CLERK: Hi, so you need a price check on a trash can?

CASHIER: Yes, it's the 33-gallon trash can.

HOME AND GARDEN CLERK: Is it the aluminum one or the plastic one?

CASHIER: It's the plastic one.

HOME AND GARDEN CLERK: Right, that's $10.99 for the plastic trash can.

CASHIER: Thanks.

Activity #2—Student Text Page 81

EVA: Hi, Hiroshi.

HIROSHI: Hi, Eva. We need to check the stock numbers for today. Are you ready?

EVA: Sure. You read the list, and I'll check the boxes.

HIROSHI: OK. Number one is A 16 002.

EVA: Let's see. A 16 002. Yes, it's here.

HIROSHI: Next is E 70 013.

EVA: I think that's over there. Yes, E 70 013.

HIROSHI: The third number is Z 14 035.

EVA: Z 14 035?

HIROSHI: Right! then we need I 18 067.

EVA: I think that's under this box. Here it is. I 18 067.

HIROSHI: Now we're up to number 5. It's B 15 012.

EVA: B 15 012. I don't see that one. Circle it on the list and I'll ask Mrs. Nelson about it.

HIROSHI: Number six is N 19 064.

EVA: Yes, N 19 064 is right on top. What's next?

HIROSHI: Next is P 50 025. Do you have that one?

EVA: I think so. Yes, here it is. P 50 025.

HIROSHI: We are almost finished. Our last number is E 60 302.

EVA: E 60 302. OK that's here too. Great. I'll give the list to Mrs. Nelson.

Unit 9—Listening
Activity #1—Student Text Page 91

LEROY: Hi, Gilberto! How are you?

GILBERTO: I'm fine, thanks. How about you, Leroy?

LEROY: I'm okay now. I was sick last week, but now I feel better. I know I wasn't eating very well, so now I want to eat more fruits and vegetables. I think I will feel better. I also want to start exercising every day. I think I can exercise for 15 minutes every morning before I come to work. With more exercise and healthy food, I know I will stay healthy.

GILBERTO: That sounds great, Leroy. I'm glad you set some goals for yourself. Here, I'll even give you my apple for lunch.

LEROY: Thanks, old buddy. I have another goal too. I want to be Elmwood Hospital's Employee of the Year for this year. I think my supervisor wants to recommend me. That's why I'm so happy today. You look pretty happy today too. Tell me why.

GILBERTO: Well, I set some goals too, and now I'm working towards them. I want to get a promotion and make more money here at the hospital. I am also trying to save more money. I need a new car. With the money I have, I think I can buy a car next month. I also plan to take my first class in laboratory technology next week. It will take a couple of years, but I am sure I'll get my degree. Maybe you and I will work together in the lab.

LEROY: I'd like to work with you in the lab someday, Gilberto. If you need any help studying, let me know.

GILBERTO: Thanks, Leroy. My break is over, so I have to get back to the floor. See you later.

LEROY: OK, see you later.

KIM: Hi, Jenna. Sit here with me.

JENNA: Thanks, Kim. I'm so hungry today.

KIM: But you don't have much to eat—only a little apple.

JENNA: Yes, I'm trying to lose weight. I want to lose ten pounds. I set a new goal for myself. I want to travel to a foreign country on my vacation, and I want to lose weight before the trip.

KIM: That sounds like a great idea, Jenna. You look like you need a vacation.

JENNA: I do. I am trying not to work any more overtime. Another goal I have is to have more free time. I like making extra money working overtime, but then I don't have time to see my friends, to work on my math homework, or to clean my apartment. I want to take another math class next semester. I really like studying math.
How about you, Kim? Do you want to take any classes next semester?

KIM: Yes. There are two classes I want. One is an English class. I want to learn to speak more English. The other class is a computer class. I like computers and I want to know more about them.

JENNA: Registration for next semester starts in two weeks. We can go together to register if you like.

KIM: That sounds great, Jenna. I need to save more money for my classes, so I am working all the overtime I can get. I have to get back to work now. I'll see you later. Then we can talk more about our classes for next semester.

JENNA: Sure, Kim. I'll see you later.

Activity # 2—Student Text Page 92

(This is a telephone conversation.)

APPLICANT: Hello. Can you give some information about the position available for a nursing assistant?

PERSONNEL OFFICER: Yes. We now have two positions available for nursing assistants.The nursing assistants report to Mrs. Olivia Armstrong.

APPLICANT: How much experience is needed?

PERSONNEL OFFICER: You need 3 years' experience as a nursing assistant for this position.

APPLICANT: Can you tell me about the benefits, please?

PERSONNEL OFFICER: Yes. There are 9 paid holidays every year. There are also 2 weeks of paid vacation.

APPLICANT: Thank you. What are the hours and the salary?

PERSONNEL OFFICER: The nursing assistants work from 6:30–2:30 and the salary is $18,000 a year.

APPLICANT: Thank you very much. How can I get an application?

Personnel Officer: You can come to the personnel office in the hospital Monday through Friday from 9:00–5:00.

APPLICANT: Thank you again. Good-bye.

PERSONNEL OFFICER: Good-bye.

Unit 10—Listening
Activity #1—Student Text Page 101

Clara is in the company lunchroom. She is eating lunch and reading the company newsletter.

JOE: Hi, Clara. Mind if I join you?

CLARA: No, Joe. Have a seat. I'm reading the new issue of "Painting the Town".

JOE: What's "Painting the Town"?

CLARA: It's the name of Rainbow Paints' company newsletter. Each employee receives a copy every month.

JOE: I started working here only three weeks ago. What does the newsletter say?

CLARA: This newsletter is titled "You're never too old to learn."

JOE: I don't believe it. Learning and school are for kids.

CLARA: You won't say that after you read this. Look.

JOE: *(reading from company newsletter)* Let's see. It says, "Rainbow Paints is more than a factory, it's also a school inside of a factory. There are many opportunities to learn without leaving the building. For example, every employee receives training for his or her job during their first weeks on the job. Think of this training time as learning while you earn."

"In the next few weeks, every employee will receive another opportunity to learn while working. Beginning next month, Rainbow Paints' employees will use new computers to keep track of orders, production, and supplies. Even the next copy of "Painting the Town" will be done on the new computers. To help teach all of us to use the new computers properly, an instructor from CompuTech, the computer company, will be here for the next two weeks. The instructor will give each supervisor a schedule of the times and dates for the classes for the employees in each department. Employees who want more time to practice using the computers may come to the lunchroom before or after their shift, or during their lunch time."

CLARA: See, Joe. Everyone can learn something new here. And it's good to know how to use a computer. So many companies are using them that we must use them too if we want to be competitive and keep profits high. If the profits decrease. . .

JOE: I know, I know. If the profits decrease, we can lose our jobs. I guess you are right, Clara. Computers are important for the future. My son and my daughter are learning how to use them in school. But I'm 40 years old. I still think I'm too old to learn something new like computers. It's fine for someone young, like you.

CLARA: Joe, I was afraid of the computers, too. But I talked to my supervisor, and now I feel better. In fact, I'm ready to start classes right now. Besides, you are never too old to learn.

JOE: How do you know that, Clara?

CLARA: Because it says so right here in the newsletter. *(Both Joe and Clara chuckle.)*

Skills Index

The skills listed below are introduced and/or emphasized on the pages indicated.

Cooperative Learning Skills

Completing a conversation, 3, 13, 66, 76
Creating role plays, 4, 13, 26, 37, 47, 56, 76, 87, 97
Discussing appropriate and inappropriate topics of conversation, 36
Discussing positive work attitudes, 6, 14, 15, 25, 56, 57, 59, 66, 76, 98
Discussing prices, 40
Discussing problems, 1, 3, 4, 8, 25, 26, 52, 56, 57, 58, 76
Discussing unsafe working conditions, 25, 26
Discussing valued work behaviors/qualities, 62, 66, 76, 79, 88
Expressing opinions, 4, 14, 15, 22, 28, 66, 76, 79, 87
Introducing people, 47
Prioritizing goals, 88

Critical and Creative Thinking Skills

Analyzing motives for actions, 55
Analyzing personal strengths and weaknesses, 76, 79
Completing a conversation, 3, 13, 66, 76
Creating role plays, 4, 13, 26, 37, 47, 56, 76, 87, 97
Differentiating facts and opinions, 87, 97
Establishing criteria for evaluation, 66, 76, 78, 87, 88
Judging appropriate and inappropriate topics, 36
Judging criteria for evaluation, 79
Judging if sufficient information is given, 65
Judging reasons for tardiness, 4
Judging polite and impolite statements, 14
Judging statements that accept criticism or reject criticism, 56
Prioritizing goals, 88

Functional Literacy Skills

Reading a company memo, 48, 49, 89, 99
Reading a company newsletter, 67
Reading a company policy manual, 5
Reading a list of steps to solve problems, 57
Reading a posted job opening, 89
Reading an employee's checklist, 15
Reading an employee evaluation form, 78
Reading and understanding abbreviations, 15, 27, 37, 38, 39
Reading employee notices on the bulletin board, 38
Reading safety signs and labels, 25, 27

.ing appropriate responses in work situations, 4, 56, 58, 59
.tiating numbers, letters, and names, 30, 37, 38, 40, 80, 81, 92
.fying a speaker from context clues, 7, 17
.ning for prices, 40, 50, 80
.ening for specific information, 7, 8, 16, 29, 30, 40, 50, 59, 69, 80, 81, 91, 92, 101, 102
.istening to a customer's order in a restaurant, 16
Listening to a list of hotel amenities, 50
Listening to identify personal goals, 91
Listening to safety instructions, 29
Listening to radio traffic reports, 8
Understanding context clues, 7,29, 69
Using auditory discrimination, 69, 81

Literal and Inferential Comprehension

Checking literal comprehension, 2, 12, 15, 24, 35, 39, 45, 49, 55, 65, 68, 75, 79, 86, 90, 96, 100
Establishing prior knowledge, 1, 10, 21, 33, 42, 52, 62, 72, 83, 93
Expanding vocabulary, 2, 5, 11, 12, 14, 23, 27, 34, 37, 44, 48, 54, 57, 55, 64, 67, 74, 77, 85, 89, 95, 98
Identifying characters' feelings and attitudes, 3, 12, 35, 72, 75, 86, 96
Identifying new words and phrases in context, 2, 5, 11, 12, 14, 23, 27, 34, 37, 38, 44, 48, 54, 57, 64, 67, 74, 77, 85, 89, 95, 98
Making inferences, 1, 6, 10, 24, 28, 35, 39, 42, 45, 55, 62, 65, 72, 75, 87
Making predictions, 1, 10, 21, 32, 42, 55, 62, 72, 75, 96
Reading fictional stories, 2, 11, 22, 33, 43, 53, 63, 73, 84, 94
Relating experiences to reading, 1, 6, 10, 15, 21, 32, 36, 42, 46, 47, 52, 56, 58, 62, 66, 68, 72, 76, 83, 93, 98
Sequencing and prioritizing information, 16
Using and understanding new words and phrases, 2, 5, 11, 12, 14, 23, 27, 34, 37, 38, 44, 48, 54, 57, 64, 67, 74, 77, 85, 89, 95, 98

Math and Graphical Literacy Skills

Adding decimals, 18, 19, 20, 41, 51, 82
Adding whole numbers, 31, 51, 71
Calculating percentages, 18, 19, 20, 31, 61, 103, 104
Changing decimals to percents, 61
Changing percents to decimals, 104
Completing a chart, 9
Determining which operation to use to solve a problem, 51, 92
Dividing whole numbers, 92
Estimating numbers, 41
Interpreting a bar graph, 30, 31, 70
Interpreting a line graph, 60
Interpreting a pie chart, 103, 104
Multiplying decimals, 18, 19, 20, 51, 82, 92
Multiplying whole numbers, 71, 92
Plotting information on a bar graph, 105
Reading a chart, 9
Reading a paycheck stub, 81, 82
Subtracting decimals, 51, 82
Subtracting whole numbers, 9, 31

Problem-Solving Skills

Accepting or rejecting criticism, 56, 59
Applying problem-solving skills to new situations, 58
Differentiating appropriate and inappropriate conversational topics, 36
Differentiating facts and opinions, 87, 97
Differentiating formal and informal names in the workplace, 46, 47
Differentiating polite and impolite statements, 14
Differentiating statements that accept criticism or reject criticism, 56
Evaluating reasons for tardiness, 4
Introducing people, 47
Investigating an error on a paycheck, 47
Offering suggestions for promotions, 87
Prioritizing goals, 88
Sequencing emergency procedures, 26
Solving a puzzle, 54
Suggesting additional safety signs in the workplace, 28
Suggesting solutions to safety problems, 25, 26, 28

Speaking Skills

Discussing appropriate and inappropriate topics of conversation, 36
Discussing consequences for tardiness, 4, 6
Discussing facts and opinions, 87, 97
Discussing formal and informal names, 46
Discussing the need for job training/continuing education, 93, 97, 98
Discussing positive work attitudes, 6, 15, 76, 79, 87, 88
Discussing prices, 40
Discussing restaurants, 10
Discussing safety signs and labels, 28
Discussing tardiness, 6
Discussing traffic jams, 1, 8
Discussing valued work behaviors/qualities, 66, 76, 79, 88
Evaluating an employee, 76, 78, 79, 87
Evaluating yourself, 76
Expressing opinions, 4, 15, 21, 25, 28, 66, 79, 88
Giving and receiving suggestions for work improvement, 56, 87, 97, 98
Identifying unsafe working conditions, 25
Introducing people, 47
Prioritizing goals, 88

Writing Skills

Completing a cloze exercise, 8, 100
Completing a form with job information, 90, 100
Completing a memo, 49
Completing a recommendation form, 68
Completing an order form, 49
Constructing sentences with frequency adverbs, 6
Constructing sentences with imperatives, 16, 28
Constructing sentences with present tense verbs, 6, 16, 28, 45, 79
Copying safety signs and labels, 28
Writing abbreviated messages in sentences, 39
Writing prices, 40, 41, 80
Writing questions, 36
Writing sentences about personal strengths and weaknesses, 79
Writing sentences to state problems, 58
Writing solutions to problems, 58